Hearts of Light

and a

Mother's Vision of Love

Grieving with Grace

Vicki Reccasina-Malloy

1st WORLD
PUBLISHING

Hearts of Light and a Mother's Vision of Love

Grieving with Grace

Vicki Reccasina Malloy

Copyright © 2022 Vicki Malloy

Published by 1st World Publishing
P.O. Box 2211, Fairfield, Iowa 52556
tel: 641-209-5000 • fax: 866-440-5234
web: www.1stworldpublishing.com

First Edition

Library of Congress Cataloging-in-Publication Data.
ISBN Softcover: 978-1-4218-3529-7
ISBN Hardcover: 978-1-4218-3530-3

This material has been written and published for educational purposes to enhance one's well-being. In regard to health issues, the information is not intended as a substitute for appropriate care and advice from health professionals, nor does it equate to the assumption of medical or any other form of liability on the part of the publisher or author. The publisher and author shall have neither liability nor responsibility to any person or entity with respect to loss, damages, or injury claimed to be caused directly or indirectly by any information in this book.

TABLE OF CONTENTS

I REPRESENT YOU

Dear Jai,

After your death I felt like a volcano erupting forth with endless memories, thoughts and feelings for you. As I was going through the many chapters of our time together I needed to find some form of expression from the barrage of impressions that was left behind from your life as my son. If I didn't have the outlet of bringing my pen to paper, I think I would have exploded.

I was pregnant with you for nine months and on the auspicious day of your birth, you entered into the world. Since you died I am birthing you once again, only this time in spirit, the spirit of Justin through highlighting the many characteristics of who you were as my son. Your essence is what remains, now celebrated in a different form. The body that housed your soul is gone, but your eternal nature is still with me, and I am letting your voice be heard through mine. I am here to represent you and give rise to your memory, waves on the ocean of our love moving forth from the depths of my being.

It is my honor and absolute joy, and I thank-you for this privilege.

I love you,
Mom

For Justin Edward "Jai" Malloy

August 11, 1987 - June 30, 2019

Thank you for coming into my life and giving me
the gift of being your mother.

INTRODUCTION

My dear son, Justin "Jai" died very suddenly on June 30, 2019.

I texted my son that morning, "When can we talk again?" Our conversation had been cut short the day before. He texted back, "I'm slammed with work. Let's connect later on in the day."

Later on never came.

His friend and business partner found him lying lifeless at the bottom of his filled pool. My son and his girlfriend had just moved into this new house. His girlfriend was out of town that week visiting her parents.

Jai was in the backyard working on his laptop. His friend went into the house to talk on his cell phone and to get a glass of water. He said the last time he saw my son he was sitting on the ledge of the pool working. When he came out ten minutes later, Jai had drowned.

Months later the autopsy report came back that the cause of death was due to drowning, but they also found that he had an enlarged heart. We were surprised to hear that. We spoke with a heart specialist and he surmised that my son most likely had a momentary dysrhythmia of the heart and ended up passing out and unfortunately being by water created the perfect storm for drowning.

He appeared to be the picture of perfect health and nothing like that was detected, but at the same time we weren't looking for any heart problems in someone so young. Why would anyone check for an enlarged heart if there were no outward signs?

The next day I started journaling to Jai through text messaging him. After doing that for a while I decided to start writing in my journal on a regular basis as a way to stay in touch with him, heal my broken heart, and most importantly, pay tribute to a beautiful young man. It has also been a time of great inward reflection for me on my life with my son, our love, his death, parenthood, God, and heaven.

My wish is that anyone who has loved and lost a dearly beloved person can find comfort and strength from these writings, no matter what the loss.

The profound love I have for my son is the love a parent has for their child, but at the same time my love transcends all boundaries and goes beyond my own grief and embraces anyone mourning a loss.

With all love,
Vicki Reccasina-Malloy

COUSIN MEARA'S POEM TO JUSTIN

For my Cousin Justin. June 30, 2019

He is still sprouting like a grain of wheat,
very soon you will all meet.

I try to see him in the clouds,
but he is always here, right now.

He wishes you to see him from the bottom of his heart,
but please believe he is here, never apart.

And remember when he was eight,
you know that his visions were very great.

Think of his traits-nice and kind,
and also, very, very strong in the mind.

Impressive, he was blazing like a flame,
everyone now will remember his name.

Love,
Cousin Meara
Age 11

DIVINE GUIDANCE

Dear Jai,

It's Friday, July 12, 2019. I'm standing on the stage in the Civic Center with my broken heart, and your sister by my side. There are many hundreds of people here: family, friends, well-wishers, and acquaintances. They have come to mourn your death and pay tribute to your life.

Today, my dear son, is your Memorial Service.

My eulogy is a story you shared with me when you were ten years old. You had just finished your daily meditation, and you tell me that something interesting happened. For some reason I thought I should write it down. I run and get a notebook and start writing as you articulate very clearly and patiently to me your detailed vision. You say, "I am coming out of a pool of water into a dark cave. I feel a cool breeze on me, when suddenly a beautiful lady appears. I think She is a Divine Goddess: stars all around her, and in her deep, sky-blue eyes. She seemed to be a part of everything. Her complexion is paper smooth. Gemstones decorate her head, forehead and neck. I recognize a blue sapphire between her eyes. She is wearing long necklaces of pearls and other colored gems. The lady says to me, "Go to the light." I travel through a dark tunnel and come out on the other side into the light. I see all these gods and goddesses. They are in a circle, floating above me. They seem to be in deep meditation.

Most of the gods are young men, but there are ancient looking ones with long white beards. They all have divine weapons slung over their shoulders that look like little missiles. Their muscular arms are decorated with jewelry. They are powerful warriors. The goddesses are wearing long, flowing dresses made of real flowers. They have on earrings, necklaces and bracelets with many gemstones. They are very beautiful."

I ask you, " Who is the lady telling you to go to the light." You say, "Mom it's the lady in the painting on the table in your bedroom." I find the picture. It's a small, blue watercolor of Divine Mother, Saraswati, the Goddess of knowledge and music. It's a plain painting of Her with Her Vina, not like the elaborate depictions that I usually see or like the vision you had. I'm surprised you know who She is. We never spoke of Her.

I didn't know back then what to make of this experience, not until 21 years later on the day you drowned.

It became quite clear to me.

I truly believe that you were being guided by Divine Mother. Dying so suddenly can be very confusing. She was there to give you guidance of what to do to keep moving forward on your journey.

In your meditation, She planted in your awareness the knowledge to go to the light when the appropriate time would arrive. Like a caring Mother, she was looking out for Her child. My heart swells with waves of love for the Divine Goddess, Saraswati, for taking care of you when I couldn't.

I am grateful each and every day that as tragic as it is that you died, you were blessed to have the guidance of Mother to help you continue on your cosmic adventure into the heavenly realms.

I wish you were here to tell me the rest of the story.

I do think it is far from over.

Love,
Mother

SERVICES

My dear love,

August 9, 2019

Remember in 2018 when you participated in the funeral service for my mom, Nana, as you affectionately called her? The officiant needed someone to help administer sacred rites over her deceased body and we all felt you should do it.

Nana was just shy of her ninety-third birthday.

The ceremony was from an Eastern Indian tradition where a ritual is performed to honor the dead and bestow blessings for the souls' transition into the next life. It was also a preparation for the cremation of my mother's body. This was a new experience for you and I could tell that you were deeply moved by it.

Little did I know that a year later we would be officiating over your body, performing the same Eastern Indian rites for the dead. You were thirty-one years old.

Holy Gold Almighty, how strange life can be!

I look back and ask myself, "How did I get through all of the services we had for you when you died?" These were big events that needed good planning. I thank God we had a small army of devoted friends and family that pulled together the endless details: picking up out of town guests from the airport and finding housing, hiring caterers for the evening dinner we hosted for over one-hundred of your friends and family, desserts and beverages for six-hundred attendees after the memorial event, flower arranging, engaging musicians for the services and lining up speakers to eulogize you.

The first service was an evening viewing of your body at the

10

funeral home. Lines of mourners extended out the door and down the street. It was a packed parlor.

Dad, Kelly and myself stood at the front of the room absorbing wave after wave of love from the outpouring of sweet, heavenly nectar from the well-wisher's tender hearts. Love was overflowing and I felt so high that a part of myself spontaneously stepped back and silently witnessed this act of love in motion. Seeing many of your broken-hearted friends and family and the impact of your death, made me realize the importance that the service provided. This was a moment that gave everyone that cared about you the opportunity to express their feelings. It was a vital part of the collective grieving process and gave a sense of closure: a much-needed soothing salve when such a loss is experienced.

The next morning was your funeral. There was a guitar instrumental quietly playing in the background as mourners entered the home. They viewed photos: moments that captured the many phases of your growth, from your adorable cherub baby stage into your adult years as a handsome young man. People said how much they liked your pen and ink drawings, and they had no idea you were an artist. The tables were decorated with a large variety of floral arrangements: lilies, roses, salvia, zinnias and lush green plants. The room was pungent; the scent of nature wafted through the air.

Your Aunt Sharon read a lovely poem, and good friend, Carmen, read from spiritual texts.

Part of the Eastern Indian tradition was anointing your body with special oils such as frankincense and sandalwood, and the placement of holy spices on the seven chakras (also known as energy centers), as the officiant was splashing purified water over you. Her voice was filled with power and determination as she began chanting a mantra over and over, for your soul's journey. It gave me goosebumps.

The mourners carried handfuls of colorful rose petals as they silently walked in a procession around your coffin, and adorned your body with the petals. I could no longer see your handsome face or strong youthful figure. You were buried underneath a bed of flowers as the aroma of burning incense perfumed the environment. At the end of the event another good friend, Greg, sang the deeply emotional and heart wrenching song, Ave Maria. We all cried.

People commented that it changed their lives for the better. A holy event took place that morning; a consecration of your body was carried out and in the future your ashes would be offered up to Mother Earth.

After lunch we had your memorial service at the Arts and Convention Center. Our devoted group of family and friends transformed the huge, gray empty conference room into a warm and welcoming place. Long draping white voile fabric was hung from the ceiling with little white lights dispersed throughout, creating a soft celestial glow. A large photo of you hung midair. Floral arrangements in stunning hues of pink, purple, blue, and delicate white Baby's Breath flanked the stage.

We had seating for over six hundred people and every one of them was filled. I walked up the aisle, arm and arm with your sister and dad to the front row, as those in attendance sat or stood by their seats and paid their respects as we passed by. I was no longer in my body, but became a big, unbounded force of energy. This was not about me, it was about you, my son, and so it was easy to expand with this immense feeling of love I was experiencing for you. Any inhibitions I normally have speaking in front of a large group of people, especially in my delicate state of mourning, had absolutely no bearing on my demeanor. It was a moment in my life to step it up and put the small, insecure self on the shelf.

Dad's good friend, Jamie, was the emcee and gave a powerful opening talk about love and family. He was fabulous as were the other thirteen family and friends that stood up to pay homage to you. Everyone gave an extraordinary tribute with many accolades spoken with heartfelt emotions and admiration for the man you were. The continuous theme was what a positive presence you were in everybody's life, and that you were a loyal and devoted friend to all. A memorable recollection from your good friend and former roommate, Riki: "Jai was the kind of person who would open his home to his friends, no questions asked. Whatever difficulty they were going through, they always had Jai's kind support for a place to stay and regroup. I never knew who was going to be asleep on the couch. He was such a, Leo the Lion, and loved being surrounded by his pack."

At the end of the service, I felt fulfilled that we honored you in the highest and most respectful way that you were deserving of.

Your beaming presence was felt.

I thank God for lifting me up at the lowest point of my life.

I love you,
Mother

HOLY AND PURE

Dear Jai,

Watching mothers with their young children reminds me of when you were a little boy. The many impressions of your early years are still quite vivid.

I loved how passionate you became about your interests: jewelry making, collecting Beanie Babies, Legos, tree climbing, long hikes in nature, riding your beloved moped, skateboarding, skiing, snowboarding and so much more.

Your pen and ink drawings were heartwarming and were executed with precision and simplicity. You loved it all and were very good at whatever you put your mind on.

Everything you touched in your life holds a deeper meaning for me. They have become holy and pure. A sensitive person that once lived on Earth has left his imprint on all these things. Your heavenly status has elevated them to a level of sacredness for me.

My memories of your early years are precious gems I will always hold close to my heart and treasure for the rest of my life.

Love you forever,
Mom

HEAVENLY GARDEN

My dear love,

August 18, 2019

The many trees planted and flowers received honoring the great person you were during your time here on Earth, is our symbolic offering to your heavenly garden.

Each bloom with its blossoms and tree with its leaves are layers of the depth of our unending, eternal devotion to you, along with the sweet fragrance of love emanating from our hearts.

This is our tribute to the many facets of the person you once were, the life you lived and who you have transformed into. You have uncovered the depth of our feelings, exposed and completely opened up the raw emotions of our hearts.

May you enjoy these offerings and the creation of the sacred space of devotion we hold you in.

We love loving you so deeply.

You are our amazing.

Love,
Mom, Dad, and Kelly

EARLY ON

My dear Jai,

August 19, 2019

As soon as we heard that you died, we tried to get to California as fast as we could. A dear friend from our community flew us out the next day in his private plane to Chicago.

From there we flew into the Sacramento airport. We cried the whole way.

We went to the hospital, but we weren't allowed to see your body. We were told we would have to wait a few days. The kind and compassionate doctor sat with us and told us that she examined you. I asked her if there was any foul play involved in your death, and she said," no." I realized what a difficult job she had, having to tell parents that their child has suddenly died. The day before when she called us on the phone to give us the news of your death, we went hysterical.

We finally arrived at your home. Your good friends, Pete and Shea and their pup, Kiki, were there to greet us. They took great care of us, and everyone else that drove in from out of state, and made sure we all had comfortable sleeping arrangements for the next few days. Your Aunt Sharon and David were there to help out, cooking delicious meals for everyone.

In the midst of such deep grief there was so much love being put forth. The love and care we received did help soften the shocking blow of your death. We had a full house. It was comforting to see your childhood friends arrive; they were a big part of your life.

We were out in the backyard sitting around the pool where you drowned. My feet dangling in the water as I was speaking with your girlfriend, Angelique, who had just driven in from New

Mexico with her mother, brother and cousin. As we were chatting, I became aware of a persistent nudging on the back of my head. This constant nudging wouldn't stop. I finally closed my eyes and there you were. You were saying over and over to me, "Mom I love you; I love you so much Mom, I love you Mom, I love you so much Mom." Over and over until I opened my eyes and I could no longer hear you. I couldn't believe my ears and yet it seemed so natural to hear you telling me how much you love me. Thank-you for this holy moment.

A few days later the funeral home finally informed us we could view your body. As we were walking into the room where your body was laid to rest, I suddenly ran towards the coffin. As I was running, I felt a subtle part of myself run out ahead towards you. I was no longer in my body. I stood there completely composed and expanded. I was then holding space for everyone else to view you and shed their tears. A surreal moment in time.

The next day we held a lovely ceremony at the pool for you. We passed out yellow roses to everyone present. Each person tossed their flower into the pool as they wished you a beautiful journey.

We blessed the place where you died and it felt good. This act of blessing uplifted the whole space and made it a sacred spot honoring your movement through the timeless portal of this life to the next.

Loving you beyond words can ever express,
Mother

GIVING BIRTH

Dear Justin,

August 20, 2019

I have so many delightful memories of your childhood and formative years and it all began with being pregnant with you. I always wanted to have a home birth and your birth day allowed me to fulfill that desire.

Before you and Kel were born, I lost my first baby during my sixth month of pregnancy—a baby I was planning on giving birth to in our home with a midwife and a team of backup doctors at a hospital on the North Shore of Long Island, New York. That was never meant to be. He was stillborn and I was heartbroken. Two weeks after I lost, "Baby Boy Malloy," Dad received a job offer in Iowa, and we relocated from the East coast to the Midwest.

Four months later I became pregnant with Kelly and delivered her in our local hospital. Her birth gave me back the confidence that I could have a successful full-term pregnancy. I was so grateful!

Three and a half years later you were born in the comfort of our sweet house on B Street. We had recently renovated the walk out basement so you and Kelly would have a big playroom to use when you got older, also a large family room where your delivery would take place. The space had a long row of windows and the early morning sunshine poured in and illuminated the area.

It was a fulfilling birth with the loving assistance of your godmother, Ellen, and the amazing team of midwives to help us through the process, along with an open-minded local doctor willing to be my back up. Everything went smoothly and by the book.

You were the sweetest little baby. There was a loving flow between us and I will always cherish that. Dad was so proud to have a son: to see the male extension of himself in you. Your sister became your little mother. She doted on you and cradled you in her arms. She loved you right from the start: an ancient connection of two old souls being reunited once again.

Thank you, my son, for coming into our lives.

Love,
Mom

REALIZATION

Dear Jai,

August 20, 2019

I remember being in the laundry room with you in our B Street house, you were around ten years of age. When I looked at you I felt I should bow bow down to a great presence that I suddenly realized was within you. I didn't physically bow down to you, but in my awareness I did and after that experience I gave you the Sanskrit nickname, "Jai," pronounced "Jay." In Sanskrit Jai means victory, a salutation of honor, praise and glory. The name really suited you. Most of your friends in your teen years and adult life knew you as Jai.

I noticed as you were growing and maturing, that being in your presence or in our phone conversations, I felt more expanded. You gave me deeper insights into life and the world we live in. You opened my awareness and allowed me to transcend my limitations. You always told me to be aware of my beliefs, and to discern my truths from what I am being fed by the world around me. You said to live by my instincts and realize that not everything is what it appears to be. Since you died that is certainly the truth!

You were unassumingly awesome, and I thank you for that.

Love,
Mother

YOUR ARTWORK

Dear Justin,

Your bedroom walls have become a display of your creativity, a body of artwork you created from your childhood into your teens. I love to observe the meticulous drawings you produced.

Dad did a lovely layout of your work and had everything framed. The contrast of the black frames along with the white backgrounds of your pen and ink drawings pops the figures, gestures, and expressions of your subjects and they come alive.

I noticed your skill for drawing at eight years old. You were inspired by a video series of Eastern Indian saints, sages and great heroes, along with the Indian comic books I bought you that told stories of great beings that inhabited the Earth a long time ago. Although beyond the understanding of a young boy, you had a childlike innocence and affection for these great people that lived many thousands of years ago. You admired the exemplary lives they lived and heroic deeds they performed, and you managed to capture their essence in your simple, yet detailed drawings.

As you grew into your teens your art illustrated basketball players, rappers, and abstract shapes and forms. You also maintained your love of the natural world and your sweet nature was evident in various renditions of rodents, insects and amphibians. Your drawing of a dragonfly on a lily pad alongside the red bud of a lotus flower is my favorite. Folklore says the dragonfly is a communicator from the elements and represents insights, growth, and transformation.

We feel blessed to have this part of you still with us as we enjoy and feel you through your art. It reflects an active life of discovery, as I ponder the commentary from the little boy and adolescent expressing himself through them.

Love,
Mom

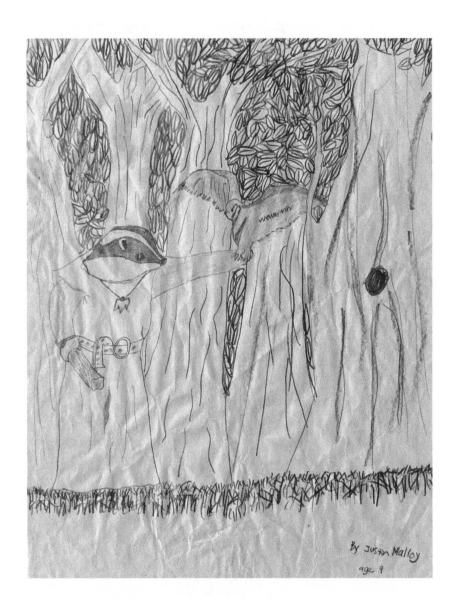

By Justin Malloy
age 9

23

CHILDHOOD TOYS

Dear Justin,

August 21, 2019

I discovered your collection of Beanie Babies and Legos in your closet. Oh my goodness, did they bring back memories!

You spent hours playing with your Legos and once you completed a set you gained a sense of achievement. The Legos were a great catalyst for your future problem-solving capabilities, fine motor coordination and giving structure to the many little parts that you created into forms. You entered into a world of childhood imagination as you constructed: astronauts flying through the universe in their spacecrafts, farmers plowing their fields on their tractors, and great warriors defeating alien monsters.

You were also a passionate collector of Beanie Babies; soft, plush toys that burst onto the market in late 1995. You loved trading them with your friends and was always on the hunt for the Beanie with the most value. You were eight years old and already I could see a future businessman in the making. They were also the inspiration behind some of the pen and ink drawings you did of little animal critters.

Geeze, I remember running all over Southeast Iowa and up to Iowa City when a new Beanie would come on the market. You had to own it so we would hop in the car and away we would go on the Beanie Baby hunt, and keep our fingers crossed that by the time we arrived at the store they would still have some in stock. You accumulated so many of these adorable soft toys; rainbow-colored Peace Bear, Rocket, the blue jay, and Glory Bear with her red and blue stars.

I recently gave away a couple of your Beanies and Legos to some of your good friends' children. The next generation that will live in their world of childlike wonder and imagination as you did. Now they have some of your special toys and a part of your childhood with them.

Loving all the beautiful memories of our life together.

Love,
Mom

MORTALITY

Dear Justin,

August 21, 2019

Your best friend recently shared with your sister a conversation he had with you shortly before you passed away. The subject matter was the mortality of your loved ones and the realization that your parents would eventually pass away, and you would be next in line to carry on the family name. The responsibility would be in your hands to bring the future generations forward. That revelation was very disconcerting to both of you.

The thought of the loss of your parents was so upsetting, you both began to sob. The torch would be in your hands and you would become the family patriarchs.

That was not meant to be for you. You died a week later.

How ironic...

Loving you so much it hurts,
Mom

TIMELINE

Dear Jai,

August 22, 2019

Which timeline of memory will I pick out today from the 31 years of your time here on Earth? I think I'll talk about the Tom Petty and the Heartbreakers concert.

Lincoln's dad offered to take a bunch of the boys to see Tom Petty on a school night. You really wanted to go. Of course, your father and I were not happy about you having to drive four hours on a school day, so we decided to compromise. We would go to the concert too; that way on the way home you could drive back with us and sleep in the back seat of the car. We brought your pillow and blanket and you agreed.

Little did we know what a great concert was in store for us. We had a blast. Tom and his band were fantastic. We all got up and started dancing to Free Falling, American Girl, I Won't Back Down and many more of his hits. The concert hall was pulsating with energy.

You got a good sleep on the ride home and all was well with parenting that evening. Chuckle.

Hey, Jai, thanks for the opportunity for a memorable night out.

I love you so much,
Mom

LANGUAGE OF THE DRAGONFLY

Dear Justin,

August 23, 2019

Since you died the dragonfly drawing you drew as a teenager carries a significant meaning for me. When this flying insect shows up I feel it is your way of communicating, through the language of nature, that you are here.

You had a love for the natural world and all its critters great and small, and the dragonfly is one of the creatures you use to say, "Hi mom, I am still with you."

In Native American mythology the dragonfly represents a time of transition and enormous transformation, along with much needed mental, emotional and spiritual growth. It also indicates a new reality from a challenging situation that has the potential to lead to Self-Realization, an opportunity to go beyond the surface and discover the deeper meaning of life.

Did your dragonfly drawing set the stage for what would take place in the future? Was this little insect and what it symbolizes a cosmic signal of your eventual transformation from a human being to a Divine being?

I do know that a time of great change was upon both of us.

I was recently sitting outside the hospital with your godmother, Ellen, waiting for valet to bring my car. Out of nowhere a dragonfly started to fly around us and then another one showed up. They began to circle around and around until one landed on Ellen and then on me. They kept this up for several minutes. Surrounded by nothing, but concrete sidewalks and cars this act of nature appeared. Your godmother and I just looked at one another. We intuitively knew it was a sign of your presence.

Please let's continue our delicate conversations. Communicating with you in this way aligns me with the divine. In this sacred space I expand to that very subtle level of gentle speech and my bliss is enlivened.

Your death is a huge evolutionary leap for me in letting go, living in the moment, and accepting what is, even though it still really sucks that you died.

Now I know what growing pains are.

I love you,
Mom

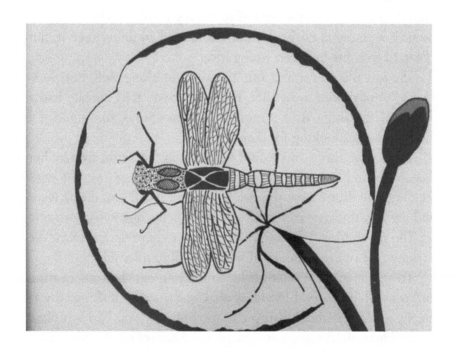

YOUR FIRST HEARTBREAK

Dear Jai,

August 23, 2019

Remember your first serious girlfriend when you were in eighth grade? The relationship lasted until you were in tenth grade. She was two grades ahead of you and right there I knew there would be trouble. I never liked the idea of you being involved with someone at such a young age. Your father and I tried to discourage it, but it's hard to come between young love.

The girl was sweet and fun and you got along well, but there was a lot of drama in her life. From what you told me she had a rocky relationship with her mother and was always running to you with her issues looking for comfort.

There were times you would tell me you felt suffocated by her neediness and weren't sure you should continue going out with her, but you didn't have the heart to break it off. You didn't want to hurt her. You also said you loved her. Such a quandary you were in. Too much for a fourteen-year-old boy to have to deal with. We encouraged you to break it off with her, all to no avail.

Two years into the relationship you found out she was cheating on you with your good friend, so that was the end of things. I was happy about the relationship ending, but now you had a broken heart. Her unfaithfulness to you, plus the lack of loyalty from your good friend, deeply hurt you.

I remember being in the kitchen with you. My arms were wrapped around you as you stood there sobbing. You told me you thought when someone tells you they love you, it's meant to be forever. I realized then, my dear son, how sweet and innocent you were about love and life.

As you grew into young adulthood I noticed your hesitation about getting into a serious relationship. Women loved you and wanted a commitment from you, but you were always honest with them and said you weren't ready.

You didn't have a committed relationship until you were 29 years old. You met Angelique, the love of your life. We also loved her and were happy you found someone that you deeply cared for and would come to spend the last two years of your life with.

Now that facet of your life has been fulfilled. That was the missing piece. You had a dynamic career on the road to success, a beautiful and loving young woman, a sweet new house and an adorable Bengali kitten mix to fulfill your love of cats.

Your life ended in fullness.

God bless you my dear son,
Love, Mom

MOTHER'S DAY SURPRISE 2018

Dear Jai,

August 28, 2019

Mother's Day became an extra special day for me. You started a sweet tradition of flying home to celebrate with me; I was so honored. I knew you had a very busy work schedule plus how long and tiring the flight from California could be, but you did it no matter what.

I remember back in 2018 I asked you if you were going to be able to get away and come home for Mother's Day. You said you wouldn't this year because you had so much on your plate at work and would come home at a later time that summer. I was disappointed, but didn't want to put any undue pressure on you, so I left it alone.

It was the morning of Mother's Day and Dad told me to go to the Rec Room because there was something there for me. I figured it was a bouquet of flowers. You always gave me the biggest floral arrangements.

As I was walking away from Dad I said to him, "I only want Justin home."

I went downstairs and didn't see anything in the Rec Room, so I went into the guest bedroom, and there you were! I began crying tears of joy. Yes, I'm an emotional Italian mother that adores her son and was bowled over to see that you came home after all. You were just kidding me when you said you wouldn't be able to make it home to celebrate. That was the best surprise of my life.

My mother was living with us at the time, and you also made her very happy. She passed away a month later.

I will always treasure that day and all the priceless memories of our life together. Saying I love you is just skimming the surface of how I feel for you, my dear son.

Love,
Mother

SITTING IN YOUR EMBRACE

Dear Jai,

August 31, 2019

My body hasn't been particularly comfortable lately, and sitting still to meditate can be a challenge. Not so the other day. I was sitting in my meditation chair when I noticed an incredible stillness permeating throughout my physiology. It felt wonderful; I couldn't feel my body anymore.

I felt a soft blanket of energy wrapped around my arms and then my whole body. In that moment I realized I was sitting in the lap of your embrace. The experience of peace and contentment was palpable. You were creating a soft cushion for me from the discomfort I had been generally feeling. I thank you for that, my dear son.

I thank you for your powerful presence in my life even as you reside in the afterlife. You're so far away and at times so close. It's completely mind boggling.

No matter what form we are, in or out of a human body, one thing that doesn't change is our love for one another; it is infinite and eternal.

Love,
Mom

FATHERHOOD

Dear Jai,

Your childhood best friend Beau, who is now a father, was visiting from out of town, and stopped by yesterday with his wife and two small children. I enjoyed watching their parenting skills. He and his wife were kind and patient with their active two-year-old son and tender and nourishing with their infant. Your friend sat with the baby in his arms while he slept. The toddler was squirming around in his mother's arms as she was gently allowing his movements while embracing him. I gave him an ice pop and that seemed to settle him.

I was holding back from crying through most of the visit. It seems every time I see one of your buddies, it reminds me of you and where you would be in your life, if you were still alive. My heart can't help but break.

I notice a particular style and quality of behavior you and your friends seem to display, and I feel your spirit: your similar sense of fashion, certain mannerisms, the millennial interpretation of spirituality, your natural goodness and sense of humor, your interests and your mode of being your authentic selves.

I also feel when a group of us are together the magnification of the love we radiate to you, is enhanced and returned back to us.

I decided to give their little boy one of your childhood toys. It was one of your beloved race cars; black and yellow with the #11 on it. His parents said, "This is from your Uncle Jai." I nearly lost it.

I'm glad you met their toddler before you passed away, and he has one of his Uncle Jai's toys.

Loving you so much with a heavy heart,
Mother

GRANDMAS' BIRTHDAY

Dear Jai,

September 1, 2019

Today is Grandma Malloy's birthday. Dad went to honor his mother and celebrate her 88th birthday with her and his sisters.

I stayed home and have some friends visiting. We're having a fun time binging on House and Garden television and watching our favorite movies like, Field of Dreams. Having time with my girlfriends is nourishing to my soul.

Dad didn't tell Grandma that you passed away. With her dementia it would be too much for her mind to handle, and the doctors don't encourage it either. They feel the shock could accelerate the disease. She may not even remember you, but either way we want to keep her innocent and in her happy world. She is quite content these days. I've never seen her like this, none of us have.

The interesting thing is that when she was speaking with Dad, she suddenly said to him that she felt like something had happened. Dad was stunned and immediately changed the subject. We always knew Grandma had good intuition and dementia hasn't changed that.

When she eventually transitions, she'll see you on the other side and oh boy; what a surprise she will have!

Love you,
Mom

MEMORIES

Dear Jai,

September 5, 2019

I close my eyes to sleep and images of your life dance before my screen of consciousness like a slide show.

I see you when you were a little baby. Kel and I were in your bedroom playing with the hanging light string in your closet. I was holding you up so you could grab onto it and pull the string to turn the light on and off.

On and off, on and off, on and off... This went on for quite a while. You got such a kick out of it. We all laughed so hard!

There was the time we got our new puppy. You were 12 and wanted a dog. We got the cutest pup at the local pet store. A brown and white Schnoodle, (a mix of schnauzer and poodle). Her coat eventually turned all white. You, Kel and I were sitting up in bed trying to figure out a name. You and your sister decided on Jenna. Dad gave her the nick name, Swish Dog, and your cousins, Eduardo and Christian, called her, Jenna Pup.

Jenna turned out to be an incredibly sweet and loving pet. Even when visiting young children were innocently manhandling her she never got aggressive.

I see the time we were in Colorado hiking up the mountain and then stopped to take a rest. You stood there with your shirt off. The mountains were behind you and the sunlight highlighted the tattoo on your chest and down your arm: a long vine, the head of a lion, a big sunflower and Shiva's trident. Having this design on your strong and sculptured physique made you look like a Greek god.

I have so many special memories of you that are stored away in the treasure chest of my heart.

Thank you for the memories

Love you so much,
Mom

ASHES TO ASHES

Dear Jai,

September 5, 2019

We sent your ashes over to India. Our friend Amit has a father who lives there. Upon receiving your ashes, his dad, Mr. Hooda, then arranged to have an Indian priest (called a Pandit), accompany him to the Holy Ganges River to spread your ashes in the water. They mingled with the ashes of millions of other great souls.

We kept some of your ashes and put them in a pond you spent a lot of time at in your youth. We also planted them at your Aunt Denise's memorial site on campus where some of Pop-Pop's and Nana's ashes are as well.

Kelly was also given some of your precious ashes. She flew out to California to spread them in the Pacific Ocean. A big group of your friends that live in Santa Cruz were present, and they all walked along the seashore to honor and pay tribute to you, my dear son, as Kelly sprinkled them into the vast blue ocean. Many hearts were breaking that day.

We received a video from Mr. Hooda of the ceremony he was performing in your honor. The Pandit was directing him to chant sacred invocations as he placed himself in the water along with your ashes. He repeated special prayers for your soul. Your handsome photo was on display. There was much laughter and happiness in the atmosphere at the Ganges ritual. I was glad to hear that. I felt it reflected your joyful heavenly status and that made me feel better.

You came into the world a plump, beautiful, angelic looking baby boy and all that was left in the end was a bag of gritty ashes.

Holy God Almighty! Suddenly it all feels like one big cosmic joke that God is playing on us. A stark raving reality that hit me in the face.

I'm on a roller coaster ride of emotions.

What a life we live, eh!

Loving you so much,
Mother

FALLING APART

Dear Justin,

September 11, 2019

I had a major breakdown this morning. I laid down on the floor of the house and screamed and cried my eyes out. I was missing you beyond words can ever express. Only a shattered heart can know the feeling of this loss and the extreme grief I feel.

What precipitated this outburst was a conversation I had with you a couple of months before you passed. I told you that Dad, Kel and myself were going through a really hard time. We each had some big challenges that we were dealing with, and it was intense. I told you that at least things were going well with you regarding your health, work, finances and personal life. A couple of months later you suddenly die. Here I am thinking all was going well with you and even told you to keep on holding it together for the rest of us and then you end up dying. One minute your life appears to be perfect, but hidden behind that illusion is a huge tragedy waiting to be unleashed.

How fucking ironic! I guess a major shit show was taking place for the whole Malloy family.

Today is also 9/11. The tragic day when so many lives were lost due to the terrorist attack in New York City. Many families around the country are grieving the loss of their loved ones.

I'm experiencing my own personal 9/11 today and also feel the sadness this day represents for our country. It's a day of mourning and the burden of grief is weighing heavy on me.

Love,
Mother

LOYALTY

Dear Jai,

September 12, 2019

I'm reflecting back to your teen years. There were some wild times! One incident was the night you and your friends were out partying. You went over to someone's house whose parent was away for the evening. Everybody at the party was drinking. One of the kids was chugging a bottle of hard liquor. This was of much concern to you and their friends. They ended up in a state of alcohol poisoning.

Your friend called the ambulance. All the kids left the house for fear of getting busted for underage drinking. Not you. You wouldn't abandon a friend in their time of great need, even if it meant you would get in trouble with the law.

The ambulance arrived and took them to the local hospital and the E.R. doctor pumped their stomach. Thank God.

A few days later a meeting was held at the police station. The kids, their parents, and the police had a talk about the dangers of underage drinking, and the irresponsibility that drinking in such excess can pose. Everyone was grateful that a life had not been lost.

To me, Justin, you were a hero that night. You put your friend's welfare before your own. You were a person of great integrity and courage, and a good buddy.

Memories of your life are passing through my mind in snippets of time as they melt away into the great continuum of infinity.

I love you so much my dear beautiful boy, Justin Jai.

Much Love,
Mother

LOVING YOU

Dear Jai,

September 14, 2019

Every moment of each day is a moment of loving you. My heart is singing with a love that goes beyond the world I am living in. Since you passed away, this feeling has affected me and how I go through my life. Anything I do: walking, talking, running errands, being with friends, strangers, and acquaintances, reading, writing, eating, drawing, meditating has the presence of you all around it.

I find myself in a new reality. At times I break down and deeply grieve your passing, other times, I feel quite large and expanded, as though I am walking with a benevolent angel by my side.

When you were alive, I had the same experience when I would spend time with you. I was aware of something bigger than what the eye could see. People couldn't help but notice you. You had good looks, but there was something beyond that, and I don't think they were aware of what it was. You always had a big, but silent energy, radiant light and a lot of charisma, broad shoulders, a warm smile and a friendly demeanor: a magnificent being. That was you then and now you fully embody your true identity.

Loving you for all eternity,
Mother

SOME OF MY TRUTHS

Dear Justin,

September 18, 2019

Everything in life feels more awake because of your passing and your heavenly presence is reflecting upon it. As you have moved beyond this life, I have also moved beyond something, but I'm still in my body so my changes are internal.

Since you died some of my truths needed to be updated. A more realistic approach to life is dawning on me. Some of these truths: My life is always growing and changing and big shocks can get thrown in along the way, like your sudden death, so I will continue to learn to take it as it comes. I know a lot about life, but I still have a lot to learn. Signs and omens are always there hinting at the future. We can be here one minute, so present, human and fully alive and then gone the next which has led me to the realization that things are not always what they seem to be. I am the creator of my reality. I have the free will to make the best out of the most difficult situations. Love transcends all boundaries.

I love you,
Mom

MY NEW ACTIVITY

Dear Jai,

September 18, 2019

Writing to you every day or as often as possible, has become a special activity of mine, my sacred time with you: a time of communicating my memories of your life and the gratitude and love I feel that accompanies these memories. It's an intimate time of silent reflection.

As I'm going about my daily activity and suddenly think of my quiet time of writing to you, it feels holy. I celebrate the divine love and unique connection blossoming between us. Subtle emotions streaming out of my heart to yours. There is something developing within me as my innermost feelings are finding an avenue of expression. Your death is giving shape to a part of myself that has been lying dormant. I suppose we are both growing in our respective worlds that we call home.

Even though you have moved through the veil of this life into the next, the thread of our love is stronger and tighter than ever.

My heart flows into yours with unbounded love and gratitude, and I thank-you for this.

Loving you forever,
Mother

YOUR INFLUENCE

Dear Jai,

September 22, 2019

We had some good friends over for lunch today. They were telling us about their daughter who is also dad's and my Goddaughter.

She decided to move from Iowa to another state to get her master's degree. She's been wanting to do this for quite a while, but was afraid to make the leap. Your passing made her realize how short life is. You proved that to many young people. Her parents said you were the impetus for her to go and fulfill this strong desire.

While we were in Santa Cruz, we spent the day with one of your very dear friends. You met in college and had an instant connection. You both had an appreciation for the outdoors, house music, good food, and loved the California lifestyle.

In response to the shock of your death he needed to unplug from the world for a while. He told us that he went on a vision quest into the forest of the Santa Cruz mountains. He camped out for several days to connect with nature and get in touch with himself and process the loss he has suffered after losing his best buddy. Being in the majesty of nature, and sleeping under the stars gave him the much-needed time for self-reflection. He felt your spirit was with him.

Justin, your life and passing has struck a deep chord within us. It's been a catalyst to decide who we are and what we want out of life and to go for it. Also, to look more deeply into the life we live and the importance to spend time in quiet reflection.

May the loving embrace of our Heavenly Mother continue to send grace and blessings to us all.

We love and miss you beyond any words can ever express, although I'll keep on trying.

Love,
Mother

MY SISTER DENISE

Dear Jai,

September 23, 2019

My sister, Denise, passed away at the age of thirty-five from an ectopic pregnancy, also known as a tubal pregnancy. She didn't know that she was pregnant.

In a normal pregnancy the fetus is supposed to move down through the fallopian tube and then develop in the uterus. Unfortunately, that's not how the pregnancy progressed for her.

Denise was experiencing severe abdominal pains. It was flu season, and not knowing that she was pregnant, assumed it was the stomach flu. In reality what happened was the fetus got stuck in the fallopian tube and as it continued to grow it started to put pressure on her abdomen and caused her much discomfort. To make matters worse she didn't have health insurance and didn't want to see a medical doctor for a diagnosis for fear of a big medical bill. Instead, she took the alternative route and continued seeing a group of chiropractors that she had been working with over the past year. Being trained chiropractors did not prepare them to accurately diagnosis her current health situation properly. They had no clue what they were dealing with, and the chiropractor with whom she had been working closely with for the past year, discarded the idea that she might be pregnant. It was assumed she had the flu and gave her herbs. The herbs masked the severity of the pain, leading her down the wrong path to wellness.

On February 10, 1986, her husband found her unconscious on the bathroom floor in their home. She was rushed to the local hospital and then air lifted to a larger hospital an hour away from us.

The doctor told us her fallopian tube had burst and she was brain dead due to the lack of oxygen to her brain from the large amount of blood loss. She still had a very faint heartbeat so they decided to put her on life support.

I decided to go and find a quiet place to rest for a bit. In this settled state, my sister appeared to my inner eye. She was floating above me in what looked to be another dimension. She had on a long flowing dress made of beautiful pink roses that were actually living, breathing flowers! Her dark brown hair, long and flowing caressed the living roses that enveloped her. The same stunning locks of hair she had as a child were now part of her celestial form. Her delicate little feet had on a pair of slippers that were fluttering about in the space she was hovering in. Had my sister become an angel?

Our parents flew in from New York the next day, and we decided to take Denise off of the life support system. We were devastated. She was married a year and a half and had so much of life to look forward to.

That night my sister came to Dad while he was settling into sleep. She said to him, " Tell Vicki that everything is wonderful." Dad said when she said the word "wonderful," he felt the thrill of her "wonderful," throughout his physiology.

That happened thirty-three years ago.

Up until my dear Mother passed away at the age of 92, she sobbed whenever Denise's name was mentioned. I couldn't understand why she was still upset about something that happened so long ago. Now having lost you, I know exactly what my mother was feeling. A mother doesn't get over losing her child, no matter how much time has passed. The sadness is always there, just as the love for one's child. The baby that she carried in her womb, gave birth to, and protected with her life was now gone. Denise was my mother's first-born child; her initiation into motherhood.

I'm sorry that I couldn't be more empathetic to my mom. I'm sorry that she had to lose a child. I realize now, that until one suffers a big loss, it's hard to know how it feels. You have only been gone a few months and well-meaning people have implied that with my years of spiritual development, I shouldn't be so sad. What people don't understand is that the more your heart develops, the more you feel of everything!

Jai, your passing has taught me how to care more, give more, love more, communicate more and feel the silence.

You grow me and I thank-you for that.

If you happen to meet my sister in heaven, your Aunt Denise, please tell her I miss and love her so very, very much.

Love you always,
Mother

WHAT REMAINS

Dear Jai,

September 24, 2019

Motherhood is the most important accomplishment of my life. The joy of making preparations for a new child coming into our family was exciting. I remember feeling the energy of your presence pulsating inside and around me; waves of your love flowing from your spirit. I immediately felt your male energy, so I decided to decorate your bedroom in the traditional blue and white color scheme for baby boys. Your place in our home and lives was ready for your arrival.

During my pregnancy with you, as your little body grew and rested against my abdominal wall, stretch marks formed on my skin. Like all women, I certainly didn't want to get these marks, but funnily enough they made me proud. They became a sacred symbol on my body of when your life was in its early stages of formation. They were your initials, your imprint on me in this lifetime. The closeness of you living, growing and developing into a human form inside of me was miraculous. Out of nothing a life was created. I had the honor to be a part of that miracle and I thank-you.

Now that you are gone from this planet, what remains is the memory that you were once here and so very close. I knew those marks were special back then, but now they have taken on an even deeper meaning for me.

My love for you knows no bounds.

Love,
Mother

TATTOO

Dear Jai,

September 25, 2019

As a way to honor you I decided to get a tattoo. I knew how much you loved tattoos, especially the one you had. Yours was a magnificent piece of art and although I'm not really into them, I do love a good work of art and yours was certainly that.

I asked a childhood friend of the family who is a talented artist to design me a tattoo with your name on it as a way to memorialize you. She did a lovely job drawing one on my left wrist. It says, "Jai," and below it, "Justin." Jai, being a Sanskrit word, a salutation meaning, "all glory," and the nickname I gave you when you were around 10 years old. She wrote it on an angle and used a simple and tasteful script. I was pleased with the outcome.

I must say that after she was done, I felt so high. In the tattoo parlor I saw a tall column of white light above me. It enveloped me and I was over whelmed with bliss. I knew you were letting me know you were happy with this tribute and the radiant white light was your heavenly smile pouring down upon me. I felt your presence.

It's interesting because I assumed I would be feeling emotional and most likely crying during the tattooing procedure, but instead I was elated. I realize how important it is to honor our deceased loved ones. They feel our love and send it right back to us. It lifts them up as much as it lifts us up.

To top it off your huge white Toyota Tundra truck was delivered to us today. The transport company dropped it off at Dad's workplace and he drove it home. I had to laugh when I saw a powerful looking truck with all the bells and whistles.

It was so, Justin.

Dad is going to give up his Jeep after the lease is up in a few months and will keep your truck. I like having your truck here, another part of your life that reminds us of you.

Every Friday when you were driving in your truck between Sacramento and Santa Cruz for work, you would call me and we would have nice, long conversations about life. That was always a special time for me. You were a loving and attentive son and I thank-you for those moments.

It still feels surreal that you are gone and that I'm even writing about all of this, but this is my reality now.

I wonder how this new reality of your death will take shape in the years to come, in the lives of your family, friends, and business.

Everyone is deeply heartbroken.

Loving you from the depths of my soul.

Love,
Mother

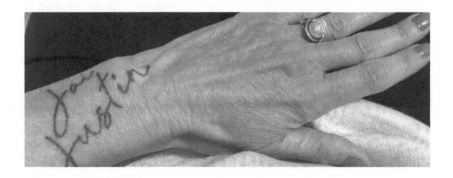

ALL MOTHERS' TEARS

Dear Jai,

As I cry, I also cry for all the mothers' that have lost a child. My tears are like an ocean flowing throughout humanity and washing over the broken-hearted grieving mother's as their tears wash over me. Our grief comes from the deepest part of what our humanity can feel.

We mothers are united in our grief.

As my tears emerge and stream out through my eyes, down onto my face, my whole body gets a chance to release the tension that was pent up inside of me. At times I don't realize how heavy the weight of this sadness is and how its been weighing me down, until it finally surrenders itself. I let go and embrace these feelings. In that moment I surrender my heart to you, my dear son, and I recognize my deep love for you.

Loving you and grieving you, happens simultaneously in this state of mourning your passing.

Loving your forever,
Mom

LEAVING IT ALL BEHIND

Dear Jai,

September 28, 2019

What was it like?

Letting go of your life here on earth and leaving it all behind in an instant. I know how much you loved us: Dad, Kel, Angelique, me, your friends, extended family, your job and the dynamic life you were living in California. You had a lovely relationship with us all and no regrets. The love was deep, rich, and full.

You were passionate about your career and bringing the cannabis industry to the forefront of acceptance with a clean, pure product with accurate scientific information. You loved culturing the plants and were always looking for a way to improve the products you were creating at the highest level of integrity, along with employing highly trained scientist to help you in this endeavor.

It wasn't just about the recreational use, which you knew I had no interest in, but you opened my eyes to how it could help people with various health challenges when used correctly. You told me about a friend that was suffering from an autoimmune disease. The doctor put her on steroids, and she gained a lot of weight and felt awful. Once she started using the cannabis tincture she lost the weight, and found that it created more balance in her condition. You allowed me to get over the judgment of how I used to view cannabis. We were both in agreement that all plants in nature serve a purpose if used properly.

As I'm viewing your life and how everything was in its proper place, I'm wondering what you went through in those final moments as your body was shutting down. There's the physical act of dying, but what about the emotional process of letting go of your loved ones? I have to think that where you were going must have felt much more charming than where you were coming from.

These are the thoughts that swim around in my head when I am overwhelmed with grief. Of course, heaven is so much more than this earthly existence and all the things I mentioned. I do believe that, but the one question plays over and over in my mind:

"Couldn't heaven wait?"

I'm missing you,
Mother

LOVE ELEVATES

My dear love,

I had to go to the hospital today to have a preliminary test before I start my radiation treatments. The test was okay. I must say, I'm becoming a pro at "Sucking it up."

A great Mahavakya that I find useful when life gets challenging is, "See the job, do the job, stay out of the misery." It gives me a powerful perspective when I need an extra boost as I'm getting into sticky areas of life and the karma is crashing down on me.

Having to compromise my way of thinking about the hazardous side effects of medical drugs went out the window with the recurrence of bi-lateral breast cancer. Now it's a matter of staying alive and trying to get another twenty years out of this body so I can be around for your sister and possible grandbabies.

The technicians at the radiation center were so nourishing, it brought tears to my eyes. These dedicated health workers are like loving angels helping people like me work through a health crisis. They were concerned that I was comfortable and did their best to keep my body temperature warm wrapping me with blankets. That's when I realized, no matter how shitty life may appear to be, as long as love and kindness is a part of it, everything gets elevated.

Thank you love and kindness.

Love,
Mom

THAT TIME OF YEAR

Dear Justin,

September 29, 2019

I'm experiencing that end of summer, September kind of emotions. The kind of feelings I used to have when you and your sister went back to school after an activity rich summer of us spending time together.

I'm remembering when you had just finished another school year of homework, deadlines, and tests, not to mention multiple after school sports: basketball, softball, tennis, and soccer. Dad and I made sure you and your sister had some, "no pressure kid time," so we made arrangements to go to the east coast.

I have visions of warm sunny days vacationing in the Carolina's and our discovery of the amazing water parks, huge water slides and wave pools. I would watch you and your sister come barreling down the slide with the look of absolute joy on your faces, and screaming with laughter! You loved the swift speed of moving through the long curving chute with water splashing all around you. You kept going back for more and more. You had a child's insatiable appetite for fun.

Next was our yearly trip to Long Island to visit our extended family. We went to Jones Beach, the place I spent a lot of my summers as a young girl. You and your cousin, Chris, had a blast together: body surfing as the waves came crashing down upon you, and eating concession stand French fries, watermelon and ice cream.

The two of you were always on the hunt to find a sea creature washed up on the shore. Remember the jelly fish you found: your ocean prize? You came running over to me so excited. You needed a shovel to scoop it up with so you could inspect it more closely before the tide took it away. You were both so proud of your capture. A young boy's delight!

Vacation time eventually came to its seasonal end and the school year was gearing up.

Today I feel the fullness of summer transitioning into winter, with autumn acting as it's liaison. Days are getting shorter and temperatures are cooling, suntans are fading and jackets coming on.

I savor the lingering flavors of our past: the memories this time of year elicits, coupled with the permanence of your death, striking an uncomfortable chord within.

It went by too quickly.

Love,
Mom

YOUR PRECIOUS RUDRAKSHA BEADS

Dear Justin,

September 29, 2019

Dad and I were with a friend today that told us something interesting about you. He said that a few days after you passed away you came to him in spirit and said, "I was referred to you." He then proceeded to give you a blessing. At the time we had no idea what this meant or what the blessing was.

Our friend spends a lot of time in India going on spiritual pilgrimages and video tapes them. He also photographs the landscapes, capturing the essence of this historic land.

We watched a video from his last journey with Indian sages and priests that he has come to know quite well, and accompany him on these special trips. It was awe inspiring and uplifting to see this ancient culture and the colorful ceremonies and rituals that are deeply ingrained in the fabric of the country. You can feel the reverence they have for God and their love of the divine in these performances.

It dawned on us when we got home that we should give him your Rudraksha beads to bring with him on his next journey to India. Your beads were always special to you and in some way seemed to be a significant part of who you were, but I had no words for why. You loved them and wore them since you were a young teen until you passed away. We called him with our request and he said he would be more than happy to bring them on his next trip. We gave him several pairs of your beads before he left town.

Once he arrived in India we started to receive texts and videos from him of your beads' journey.

The first stop for blessings was Rishikesh. The priest held your beads in his hands and chanted powerful invocations over them, immersed them in ancient rivers and anointed them with sacred oils.

The next place was Chardham Yatra with stops at the Ganges River (where your ashes are dispersed) and Yamuna Rivers. The ritual of blessings continued into the high, holy mountain temples of Kedarnath, Badrinath, Jyotir Math and Kali Math. The priest did additional blessings for Dad, Kel and me at these sacred sites.

He sent us a photo holding your beads with the Yamunotri Temple in the background tucked away in the Himalayan Mountains surrounded by green forests. The temple is dedicated to the Goddess Yamuna, the first Lady of Life. The sun was illuminating the crystals that we had strung with your Rudraksha beads. It appeared to be an offering to the ancient land.

The blessings were completed for you and your family in Kedarnath, Kali Math where five-thousand-year-old temples inhabit the region. Nearby in the town of Jyotir Math he met with the principal and staff at a Vedic College. He found out that at one time the head priest's father was the personal cook for the Shankaracharya, Swami Brahmananda Saraswati, known as Guru Dev. He was the head of the monastery and was known to be an enlightened teacher or guru. Our dear friend donated a computer and printer to the college in your name.

I believe your soul was on this pilgrimage and so was your family's. A rite of purification was being performed for all of us and we felt it.

Your family received a transcendent gift from this ancient land and we are grateful to you and our friend for facilitating this.

Love,
Mother

DEVOTED

Dear Justin,

October 1, 2019

I'm eternally devoted to you.
I'm devoted to remembering your life and
all the goodness that you brought to it.
I'm devoted to the memory of being your mother.
I'm devoted to uplifting thoughts about you.
I'm devoted to communicating with you in my
feelings, words, and daily journaling to you.
My devotion to you also allows me to grieve you.
Grieving you fully and honestly and loving you
simultaneously. I'm devoted to that too.
In this state of devotion, I fully surrender my heart
and love to you.

A special young man that lived a short, but full life,

Eternally devoted to you,
Mother

OUT OF CONTROL

Dear Jai,

October 2, 2019

Intellectually I understand that people die. Mothers and fathers lose their children every moment of of every day. I think to myself it was your time to go. This is how life played out for you and us. I believe we come into the world with a certain number of breaths. When our soul contract is up we are out of those breaths, and drop our physical form, and merge with the light of God once again. We go back home to heaven where we originally came from. Heaven is our true home.

Who knows, I still may get out of control with screaming grief, but right now it's a deep and silent sadness seeping out through every pore of my body.

Love you,
Mother

JUST JOY

Dear Jai,

October 4, 2019

I've been thinking of you today, like I do every day. I was feeling much love and joy at the thought of you and in some way, I could feel your new heavenly status. Then some sadness started creeping in, but I just couldn't get into feeling sad.

There was no room today for anything else, but just joy.

Loving you so much my dear son,
Mother

FOUR MONTHS AND FIVE DAYS

Dear Justin,

October 5, 2019

You passed the last day of June, on the 30th. Now it's four months and five days later and I'm starting to feel a little lift. I think I'll get back onto the treadmill again. I know exercise is so important especially when our emotions have been deeply impacted. Dad and Kel are also feeling a bit of a shift. I feel it's connected to whatever you are going through in the heavens and it's trickling over to us, plus it's the beginning of a new month and we are in the autumnal season.

It's one of the best seasons in Iowa along with spring. The new season seems to be erasing a little of the summer trauma, when you died.

This is the first season of the year without you in it, a different reality of something new for us to get used to.

Love you and miss you so much,
Mom

NANA'S REBIRTH INTO HEAVEN

Dear Jai,

October 10, 2019

I'm reflecting on Nana's passing. It took place on June 20, 2018 as summer was approaching. The moon was full, and she died during a special time of the morning that the Eastern Indian saints call, Navaswan: a time of profound silence in nature. It was the beginning of a new season and a new life for your Nana. She was ninety-two years old and would have turned ninety-three in six weeks.

Nana's health had been quite delicate over the last year. She was hospitalized for pneumonia and was starting to have transient ischemic attacks, commonly known as mini strokes, quite regularly. She had stopped eating and that was a strong indicator she would be transitioning soon.

I called Kelly with the news and she flew home the next day. She was Nana's first caregiver when she moved in with Dad and me. They always had a special bond.

The night before Nana passed, I decided it would be best to sleep nearby in the living room so I could listen in on her breathing with a baby monitor, in case she needed me. I was lying on the couch gazing out the windows when I saw a big, bright, white light shooting up into the dark night sky. I knew it was a sign her death was imminent. I woke around 4:00 the next morning and went into Nana's room. Her breathing was quite labored, and it was obvious she would be leaving us any minute. I woke Kelly and she ran down the stairs into Nana's room. We sat by her bedside telling her we love her, it was okay to leave, and she was going back home to heaven where her husband, daughter, parents and sister would be waiting for her. In the previous months as she was growing weaker, Nana told me that Pop-pop was visiting her during the nighttime. I felt he was preparing her for the passage from this life into the next, and that by showing himself, would bring her the comfort, and ease needed to help allay her fear of death.

Nana was taking long deep breaths, then short fast ones: long and short, long and short. This went on for several minutes; it was quite strenuous as her whole body, which was thin and frail, suddenly had this powerful pranic life force moving throughout it. It dawned on me her breathing was similar to a woman's breathing who was about to deliver a baby, preparing for the eventual transition. My mother was rebirthing to the other side. I am sure Pop-pop and the rest of her deceased family were there cheering her on and awaiting her return. They were getting ready for the grand celebration of my mom's return to her heavenly home. Nana's life was over, and her body would be left behind. In its place her radiant body of light, her soul, would be entering the celestial realms. Nana was being reborn.

Nana gave Kel and I a precious gift that morning: the gift to witness her transition. I thank my Mother for the insight I received as I was listening to her breathing, and the perspective I gained from being a part of this profound experience. These insights have given me a broader comprehension of the realities of life and death. They help put things in their proper place for me. It's a beautiful journey wherever we are going, either into or out of this earthly dimension, as we are surrounded by love, the eternal thread of life that transcends both worlds.

What a powerful play this is.

What a glorious creation God has designed.

Loving you so very much, my dear son,
Mom

ON THIS FULL MOON DAY

Dear Jai,

October 13, 2019

Dad and I walked the path by our house today with the loop trail developer. Your godmother, Ellen, was with us as well. We were looking for the best spot to put a memorial for you on the nature trail.

Ellen and her loving family gave us cast iron benches decorated with molds of bas-relief designs of dragonflies to adorn the site for your tribute. A generous local man gave us a gorgeous granite boulder with flecks of gold that run throughout it, and sparkles in the sunlight. We purchased a handsome brass plaque from a monument company in town and they inscribed a poem I wrote onto it,(please see the story, "A Beautiful Life,") and this will be bonded to the boulder. I am confident it's going to be a worthy display of honor.

We found a spot on the trail that is in the open sunshine surrounded by wild grasses, green fields, and enormous blue skies. It's the perfect place for the people walking along to sit and take a rest.

Noah's Ark will set up another memorial for you. They were so honored by all the donations that well wishers sent in your name to their animal shelter, they wanted to pay tribute to you as well.

You are one great guy: loved and missed by many.

Loving and honoring you, my dear son, is my joy.

Love,
Mom

INSPIRATION

Dear Jai,

October 14, 2019

I draw inspiration from everything since you passed: music, nature, stories, a word, a phrase, memories, people. My heart is inspired with feelings of love for you. It seems that everything good in this world is you. Your passing has deepened me and my appreciation for life and all things in creation.

The loving nature of the Justin I knew sweeps over this Earth in a way that I find incomprehensible. Your energy imprints everything I see. Who are you and where did you go that you can shine your radiance all around everything?

What an interesting path we have found ourselves on.

My heart is always bursting with love for you, and the mysteries of life and death continue to reveal and unfold themselves to me through you.

Loving you forever,
Mom

LIFE REVIEW: INFINITE AND ETERNAL

Dear Justin,

October 15, 2019

I am going through a life review with music. I'm thoroughly enjoying the tunes I grew up with as a teen back in the 60's and 70's. This was long before you were a spark of of life in my world, and yet the songs remind me of you. A popular hit was Joni Mitchell's, Big Yellow Taxi, and her plea to stop degrading the environment with chemicals. Then John Lennon's, Give Peace a Chance, a protest song against the destructive forces of war, and Jackie DeShannon's, What the World Needs Now is Love, an appeal for universal love.

It was a time of social awakening and thinking outside the box. An awareness was emerging of living in harmony with nature, ending wars and the need to love one another. This music was a huge part of the popular culture and collective thinking of my generation. These are some of the virtues you embodied and I always admired about you.

Perhaps on some level your essence has always been with me from the distant past and we have never been separated. Do we ever really leave one another? Aren't you a part of me right now and always will be?

The bond of love we share is an ancient and eternal one, passing down through the corridors of time and continuing, even now into heaven where you reside.

Is this what eternal love really means?

Moving through infinity into the 21st. century, and continuing into the celestial field of your present existence. Can anything stop our love for one another? Isn't love part of the continuum of life and nothing can ever put an end to it.

Aren't we created from love, live a life of love and go back to love when we pass on? All I can say, my dear child, as I review my life and love for you, I find that it is infinite and eternal.

Eternally loving you my adored son,
Mom

ALWAYS KNOW, MY LOVE

Dear Jai,

October 17, 2019

Always know, my love, when you felt all the pressures of the world were upon you, my heart was always there with you, quietly loving you from a distance.

Always know, my love, no matter how near or far you are from me, you are in my heart for all eternity.

Always know, my dearest son, I would do anything to have you back in our lives.

Always know that every tear I shed, I shed for the loss of you in my life in the form that I have grown accustomed to.

Always know, everything I feel in this creation, that I am feeling you.

Always know, that everything I enjoy in this creation is because I am enjoying you, my dear son, and the light you shine upon my life.

Always know, that all the brilliance in this creation, is also your brilliance that I see as an integral part of it.

On the highway of my life as the winds of change shift directions over and over again, my love is the one constant.

Always know, my love,
Mom

THE VIEWING

Dear Jai,

I went to view your body on the day of your funeral and I was surprised how fresh and handsome you looked. Your body was flown from California to Iowa twelve days after the time of your death to your official viewing, and you still looked great.

Anyone seeing you lying in the casket would have to think, what a beautiful specimen of a young man you were. On the superficial level it seems like such a waste that your masculine physique, warm smile, clear brown eyes, glowing complexion, and tall stature would no longer be present for all to appreciate. In the midst of mourning your sudden death and the shock waves I'm experiencing from this trauma, thoughts like these seem absurd and yet the human side of you is what I am attached to.

Jai, you looked so darn alive, it was surreal that you were lying there deceased. It appeared to me that in any moment you would suddenly wake up; it was unnerving.

My dear son, I truly believe that you are still alive, only now you're everywhere, in the form of golden light. Your celestial radiance is a part of the subtle beauty in the glistening sun shining through a raindrop, the rising and setting of its rays on the trees and flowers, its glowing warmth sitting on my face and all that is part of the grandeur of creation is a part of you.

You have merged with your true essence: God's essence, you have gone back home to your illuminated Self.

Love,
Mother

YOUR DEAR FRIENDS

Dear Justin,

October 29, 2019

Dad spoke to one your business partners last night. He was also a good friend of yours. We put the call on speaker so I was able to listen in.

I was deeply touched by how highly he spoke of you. He said he was always impressed with how straight forward you were in all your business dealings with potential investors, and existing ones as well. He also mentioned what an incredible hard worker you were, and a strong grounding force in the company.

While he was talking about you, your presence began to fill the room. Your spirit was profoundly felt. Jai, I believe that when you feel love coming to you from your loved ones, it's like a magnet that attracts you to us and you send it right back.

Being around your buddies brings a part of you back to me.

It's a bittersweet experience of feeling you and missing you so, so much.

Love,
Mom

THE STORY OF KRISHNA

Dear Jai,

November 13, 2019

Years ago I watched a series about the life of Krishna. He was known to be the Eastern Indian incarnation and total embodiment of God. He was a magnificent human being with all the qualities and abilities of an Avatar or God would possess. Nothing was beyond his powers. He is known for the many great miraculous deeds he performed to ease the pain and suffering of the people that were alive during a difficult time on earth.

In the Indian tradition a young boy would be sent away from home to be educated in Vedic knowledge. When Krishna and his brother, Balarama and friend Sudama, came of age, they left their family's home to go and study with the beloved teacher, Guru Sandipani. Along with the guru, his nurturing wife took care of them with the other boys in the ashram. They were a loving couple.

The day arrived when the boys' studies were completed. They were about to return to their family, when Sandipani and his wife made a special request of Krishna. Having spent time around him they recognized that he was a special soul and they had much faith in his abilities to achieve the impossible. They asked Krishna to bring back their son who had drowned. Many years ago when they were at the ocean with their young boy, the tide came in and swept him out to sea, never to be seen again. They missed him terribly and never got over the loss. They asked Krishna to please find their son and bring him back to them. He was their only child. Krishna loved his guru and wife as though they were his own parents. He promised he would find their lost child and bring him back to life.

Krishna traveled to the depths of the ocean and found out his gurus' son was taken hostage by the demon Shankhasur. The demon lived in a conch shell beneath the sea. Krishna took the conch to the Lord of death, Yama, who found the young boys' soul in the shell. Lord Yama then proceeded to blow into the conch shell, breathing life into Sandipani's son, and he was born once again. Krishna then reunited the young boy with his parents. They were overwhelmed with joy.

If only this kind of miracle could happen to you and, you could be brought back into your physical form. You would come back as a beaming, glistening ray of pure light and share your time of your heavenly sojourn with us. You could tell us all what it was like to be on the other side of life.

It's a nice fantasy and fun to dream of the impossible, when the reality of your passing is too hard to accept.

All love to you my dear, dear son,
Mom

Justin as Krishna for Halloween 3 years

SACRED SPACES

Dear Jai,

Ever since I was a little girl I liked to create devotional altars as a way to focus my love for whatever I felt was sacred to my heart. After you died I created some of these places in our home for you. I arrange objects that I feel are a reflection of you and how I imagine the heavenly place that you live in now. These altars are meant to be elegant and uplifting: an area of honor.

We turned your bedroom into a space of quiet reflection with many photos and drawings that accumulated over the course of your life. You loved crystals, so I arranged: citrine, amethyst, quartz and many others on the shelves next to your photos. Your room is a place where I like to retreat to when I want to write, cry, meditate or do whatever it is that moves me in the moment.

In the main part of the house, I have a rose-pink quartz crystal that you gave to me several Christmases ago, placed on a table along with a cobalt blue lantern that continuously glows with candlelight. I keep a variety of fresh cut flowers: roses, alstroemerias, lilies, daisies on the table along with your beloved Rudraksha beads and some of my favorite photos of you.

These are my central points of loving attention where I can admire and pay homage to you, my son, who will always live within the sacred space of my heart.

I love you,
Mom

YOUR SCENT

Dear Jai,

November 14, 2019

I was texting with your sister yesterday to find out the results of your great Aunt Frances' foot surgery. Aunt Frances lives alone and at 97 years of age she's doing pretty darn well, but could use some assistance. Kel spent the day driving her to and from the hospital.

At one point in the text I said to Kel," It's in God's hands," but instead the text read, "It's in bro's hands." In that instant I caught a whiff of your scent. I realized you were letting Kel and me know, you, her bro, was with us, and your scent verified that for me.

It was a familiar aroma of the Justin that I knew and loved as my son. The interesting thing is that I was thinking about your scent earlier in the day and couldn't remember what your signature human essence smelled like and then, it was there. It was an earthy and strong aromatic quality that belongs only to you. My senses immediately perked up. I realized that your presence was with us and you were letting us know you were watching over your dear, great Aunt Frances.

Thank-you.

Love you,
Mother

YOUR OTHER SCENT

Dear Jai,

November 15, 2019

It's another day without you here on Earth, but I got a whiff of you this morning. It was another scent of yours, different than the one I smelled yesterday. The aroma was sweeter and more fragrant, than your previous scent, yet it was a very masculine essence of how I remember you. It was subtle and quick, but undeniably Jai. Funny how I immediately recognized you and yet I never realized when you were alive you had two different fragrances coming off of you. Both of your essences were pleasant.

Putting my attention on what you used to smell like a few days ago, seems to have enlivened this aspect of your human side and a way for you to connect with me.

Thank you so much my fragrant son.

Love,
Mother

90

GRIEF

Dear Justin,

November 17, 2019

Grief suddenly stops me in my tracks, my steps become stiff, the flow of activity tense and comes to a halt. Words mid-sentence are paralyzed with the memory of your death. A mouthful of food becomes tasteless as I abruptly lose my appetite. A tear streams down my cheek and screams out, "Why did you leave us so soon?" Doubt sets in and misery takes over; in that moment life becomes unbearable. Your death feels so senseless, a total waste of a beautiful life, now gone. Signs and messages from you feel like a consolation prize, a token of all that remains of your magnificent humanity, is now a subtle imprint of the past.

I need a respite from grief, the continuous tsunami of remembering over and over and over again that I lost you, my son. My world has been shaken up, my confidence shattered and my faith destroyed. The moment of grief passes, the physical and emotional hit seems to lift, but my endless yearning and love for you grows stronger and deeper with each passing day.

I'm counting my years to where you are, and until then my heart and soul are always with you my dearest love, my child, my life.

Always loving you,
Mom

ETERNAL

Dear Jai,

How many words and pages in my journal will it take to express my adoration for you? There are many ways to articulate how much I love and miss you. Different days and numerous moments reflecting on your life. Beginning in the womb, then seeing you lying in your casket, eventual cremation and spreading your ashes in holy rivers, ponds and oceans. I'm on an endless journey of honoring you, dear Justin. It's the motor in my engine, it keeps me going, it's my joy.

My awareness lingers in the continuous observation of the young man that once was my child.

My love for you has no beginning and no end, like you, it's eternal.

Loving you forever,
Mother

UNBEARABLE

Dear Jai,

November 20, 2019

There are moments when the thought of your death becomes un-bearable. It makes me feel hopeless and powerless. I ask my God, "What can I do to bring Justin back?" "Absolutely nothing," is the reply.

I sit down to meditate and I hit a wall of grief, there seems to be no letting up. My mind and heart struggle and sitting there becomes a big strain. My body aches, I can't sit still. I try to stick it out, but after a while I realize it's best to go lie down in bed and try to get comfortable. It helps, and all I can do is wait it out and be easy on myself till it passes.

Daily journaling my love to you, spending time with dear family and friends, getting lost in a good book or movie, are all a distraction from the distress of your loss.

As Thanksgiving and Christmas are approaching, I feel your presence. The imprint of your holiday visits home is deeply ingrained in the activity of the season for me. Remnants of our past together, floods my senses and I can taste it, smell it and see it.

Remember the huge appetite you had? I would be busy cooking a holiday meal when you would come into the kitchen, starving. I would boil up chicken hotdogs to hold you over till the food was ready. It didn't seem to affect your appetite when dinner was served. Once you were fully satisfied you would lie down and take a nap. I would jokingly say, "Justin's out for the count."

The enormous amount of excess debris from the wrapping paper, bows, and boxes that came with the gift giving spirit of

Christmas concerned you. You were disturbed by the commercialism the holiday promoted and the negative impact the waste had on the environment. You encouraged me to get non-laminated paper made from recycled materials to wrap your presents in.

All these moments come alive and you feel right here with me, and yet you are so far away. It's difficult to think I'll never celebrate another holiday with you ever again. The finality of your death is a heavy burden I now bear.

Then the torturous thoughts of how I could have prevented your death, start to plague my mind. I spoke to you the day before you died and we texted the morning of your death, so maybe, just maybe, somehow, things could have turned out differently. The course of events could have changed, but they didn't. The destiny of one's death cannot be changed, if that is their true destiny. My ego feels frustrated that I have no power over this. I know it's irrational, but I'm a grieving mother and not always rational.

I was given the gift of being in contact with you in the final moments of your life, and I treasure those last conversations with my whole heart. This is what I take with me from that pivotal time of your imminent passing.

Thank-you for those last moments.

I love you so much it hurts,
Mom

MOMENTS

Dear Justin,

November 21, 2019

In my most challenging moments is where I have the opportunity to find my strength.

In those moments I see how emotionally fragile I am and that is okay since I'm grieving, but somehow, I know I must move past the sadness and pick myself up and pull myself together. In moments of my deepest lows, I need to rise up to whatever the task that is before me. I need to carry on each and every day even though at times I would just like to crawl into a corner and die. Living life is a full-time job, and without you in it, has cast a dark cloud of sadness over it.

I need to keep moving forward and continue with my meditation practice, exercise routine, creativity, listening to music, writing to you, spending time with loved ones, watching funny movies so I can laugh a lot, and always keep the bigger picture in view. Perhaps this will help me more easily accept the challenge that I am being faced with. I am certain you would want me to do this.

You proved how short life is.

Loving you in each and every moment,
Mom

YOUR BREATHS

Dear Justin,

November 23, 2019

Where are the breaths you once breathed while in human form? The inhale and exhale that are no longer part of your human beingness, now that you have become a full-time divine being. But still, where are the breaths you left behind? Are they circulating around the world, enlivening the atmosphere in other lands? Will every loving word you ever spoke containing the essence of your gentle breaths behind them, touch a suffering heart and bring comfort and peace to it?

Does someone suddenly breath in an exhalation of the remains of your human vital life force, feels energized in that second, and the courage to move forward in a challenging situation?

Will your precious breaths come full circle and travel back to me and will I suddenly feel your presence? I will breathe you in and be rejuvenated to carry on in the bittersweet emotions of loving and missing you too, too much.

I'll continue breathing, in, hopes to catch the heart of your powerful life force, your sweet, soft breaths.

Loving you,
Mother

THE SOUND OF YOUR VOICE

Dear Justin,

November 24, 2019

Where's your voice? The soft, yet strong sound that you spoke with? I heard it today when I played the video you sent me of your new home the day before you passed away. You were going from room to room showing me the layout of your place and playing fetch with your new Bengali mix kitten, Jade.

Hearing your voice seems so surreal, now that you are a discarnate being. My question remains; where did the sound waves of your own unique voice go?

Are they in heaven with you?

But, what about the remnants of the energetic imprint of your voice on planet Earth?

Are the remains of your vocal sound waves vibrating with the sounds of other voices, in unison and harmony, in loving expressions for humanity?

Will a newborn baby boy grow up and have your voice since you no longer need it?

Is the genetic blueprint of your voice, in sounds of joyous laughter ringing through me when I burst out in hysterics triggered by something I find amusing?

Is it in the sound of an audience's appreciation of laughter at your favorite comedy club?

Is your voice echoing down through the corridors of time moving into infinity?

Are the gentle whispers of your voice pulsating throughout the universe and circling back to Earth?

Dear sweet Justin, I will always be loving you and the essence of my child's voice will be reverberating throughout me for all the days of my life on Earth.

Love,
Mom

MESSAGE INTERRUPTED; LIFE INTERRUPTED

Dear Justin,

November 25, 2019

The day before you passed away you called home. I heard your voice on the answering machine and ran to the phone to interrupt the message you were leaving so we could speak. That was the last time I would talk to you.

The next day you died.

Drowning interrupted your life: a life we all thought would continue at least another 50 plus years, (according to your family's longevity), but it didn't. Death interrupted the possibility of a long life. The continuous process of living, growing, enjoying, learning, working, and being with us, all interrupted.

I do believe your essence, divinity and soul lives on and nothing can ever interrupt that. Your body was the coat you were wearing in this life to house your soul. On that fateful day, your coat came off so you could merge with the light of the Divine reality.

You were following your destiny.

Loving you for all eternity,
Mom

BROKEN

Dear Jai,

November 26, 2019

A lot of people have something broken inside of them and it's usually their heart. If they have ever truly loved someone, then at one time or another something has broken.

On planet Earth many of us are walking around with our hearts broken due to loss of a parent, child, spouse, friend, pet, and so on. We end up going through life longing for their presence. Missing the special relationship that once was, and the finality that it's gone from our life, can be too much to bear at times.

The breaking can be irreparable.

Sharing our losses with others is a strong unifier. When we suffer a great loss, we have the opportunity to be more compassionate and empathetic towards one another, no matter what our color, creed, politics or social standing because love bridges the gap. We become sensitized to a facet of the human condition and what it endures, that we may not have been aware of before.

There's beauty in the broken hearted because love is at its core. Loving you always my dear son, with a full, but broken heart.

Always,
Mom

TRIBUTES

Dear Jai,

Every word I write in adoration of you,

Every wave of love that emanates from my heart for you,

Every song I hear and sing that reminds me of you,

Every smile I smile when I think about how you did everything in a big way,

Every flower I plant in memory of how much you loved nature,

Every laugh I laugh when I hear something funny,

Every cat I cuddle that reminds me of your dear kitten, Jade, who shared the same birthday as you,

Every photo that I look at of you and admire how handsome you were,

Every impulse I have to honor your dynamic life,

Justin, know these are my tributes to you my dearest son, and the life you left behind.

This is your mother's way to continuously acknowledge the essence of Justin "Jai" Malloy and pay homage to your memory.

I love you so very much,
Mom

BLUEBERRY CAKE DONUTS

Dear Jai,

December 1, 2019

I just found out from Kelly that you loved blueberry cake donuts. Funny how the little things seem so important now. Anything new I may find out about you is like discovering a precious golden nugget that I will always cherish. I didn't even know you ate donuts. Learning new things about you, no matter how ordinary or uneventful, brings a part of you back to life. I feel your personality. It's a reminder that you were once here, alive and acting like a person, eating and having particular preferences, like us humans do. It makes you more relatable to me, and that feels good, as I am trying to get used to you as a being of light.

I used to make blueberry cake muffins with a streusel on top when you were growing up and you loved them, so I guess it carried over into donuts. Did the donuts bring back a sweet flavor of your childhood? I bet they did.

Now you are somewhere in the heavens in your celestial form, eating God knows what, if anything at all. I assume pure light and love is all the nourishment you receive in heaven now that your physical body is gone. Or since you can have anything you want, you may be eating lots of donuts till your heart's content.

I guess this is all food for thought.

Love,
Mother

AGING

My dear Jai,

You will never have to grow old. I guess that's a good thing. Watching my parents' health deteriorate was hard on them and those of us watching their yearly decline, but at the same time it was easy to accept and understand as a process of life. They lived good long lives and eventually their earthly incarnation was coming to a natural end. It's a normal part of the life cycle you won't be experiencing.

My dear one, tell me about aging when one goes to heaven.

An interesting thing happened recently to a friend of yours that is prompting me to ask. He got in touch with your sister and said he had an incredibly vivid dream of you, which I believe is a visitation. He said you appeared to him when he thought he was asleep but felt wide awake. He told your sister that you were completely enveloped in light, inside and out; you appeared as a being of light. You were about ten years old. He remembers in the vision you had the same wavy hair you had as a child at the time you first met as young friends. You grew out of the wavy hair when you became an adult.

I find it interesting you came to him in the vision at that particular age, even though he knew you in your later years. He said he felt so happy to see you and that you were doing really, really well. He told your sister he never experienced anything like this in his life. When he saw you he felt comforted.

Why did you choose to appear to him at this particular age? Is it so he could feel some sense of childhood familiarity with you?

Were you in some way more relatable to him and one he could recognize you in? Did it bring back memories of a playful time in your lives of going to the water park with your family and friends?

In a sense you have been frozen in time. Your youth, good looks, and vibrant health was never taken away from you through the aging process. I will always remember you full of life: strong, dynamic, and wonderful to be with.

It's a perfect image to have of you and one I will always cherish.

I love you, my dear one,
Mom

UNSEEN-SEEN-INVISIBLE-VISIBLE

Dear Jai,

December 2, 2019

Before you were born, I didn't know I missed you. I had no recollection of any previous times you may have been in my life. Most of my memory of previous lifetimes is deeply buried away in my memory bank. Then you were born to me and the feeling of familiarity was warm and comfortable. I felt I had already known you.

Our hearts were one once again.

You came from the unseen place of heaven into this lifetime on August 11,1987 and were seen. Now you have gone back to the invisible heavenly realms, only now I remember you, and not being able to see you saddens me. From the invisible you came for 31 years to live on this planet, became visible and I had the opportunity to know and love you. Now you are back to the unseen, invisible world.

What a life we live. What a crazy set up. I need to have a good talk with the CEO of this operation about how things are being run.

This time I will never forget you, unseen-seen-invisible-visible.

Love,
Mom

CHRISTMAS ORANGES

My dear love,

December 4, 2019

The holiday season is approaching and this is your family's first Christmas without you.

Kelly wanted to honor you with a table top Christmas spruce tree. She adorned it with little white lights, sparkly stars, a crescent moon and a variety of other holiday ornaments, topping it off with a silver letter J. A circle of oranges surrounded the base of the tree.

As soon as I saw the photo she sent me, I flashed to the time you were a baby. You were six months old and sitting in your highchair. Kelly was 3 years old. She was busy playing with oranges and decided to fill your highchair tray with them.

I took a photo of you surrounded by all of the oranges with your sister standing next to you. You were a king and the oranges your loyal subjects.

Your sister didn't remember that childhood moment with the oranges until she stood back to admire her creation.

I see a great connecting power is present when we pay tribute to the deceased. It enlivens the thread of love that exists between us and keeps us connected. Memories that are lying dormant, awaken.

This is our way of staying in touch and honoring you.

An unspoken dialogue is communicated from heart to heart.

Always loving you from the depth of our hearts,
Mom

CAUTIOUS

My dear Justin,

December 6, 2019

As a response to your passing and my experience that life can change in an instant, I have become more cautious. When I get up to walk, I must find my footing and plant it firmly in the steps laid out before me. I hope to find a progressive flow as my time on Earth continues to unfold. I tread carefully and try to prepare myself for any unknown event that may slam me back down on the slippery slope of life's highway.

Being more cautious has given me the opportunity to slow down and take the time to delve more deeply into life's mysteries.

My love for you gives me the impetus to navigate through life without you.

Always loving you,
Mom

I BREATHE YOU IN

Dear Justin,

December 6, 2019

I hold your photo to my heart; I breathe you in.

I hear your voice on the answer machine message; I breathe you in.

I reflect on our last conversation the day before you died; I breathe you in.

I go to the closet in your bedroom, put my face in your clothes; I breathe you in.

I remember the day I gave birth to you; I breathe you in.

I admire the lovely pen and ink drawings you created; I breathe you in.

I feel the warmth of the sun on my face; I breathe you in.

I honor the great man you grew into; I breathe you in.

Life has given me the breath to breathe your essence into my heart and that sustains me.

I breathe you in.

I love you,
Mom

GRIEVING WITH ENDLESS WORDS

Dear Jai,

December 7-8, 2019

I am your mother and I refuse to lose my connection to you, my son, since you passed away very suddenly. For the past six months I have been grieving with endless words to you each and every day. This is my lifeline to you. They keep me afloat on the turbulent waters of life.

Words are my silent link to you. They swell up from the core of my being, and are composed into the language that I know so I can communicate to you and to my God: love, sadness, admiration, shock, anger, gratitude and devotion in how to deal with your passing. As long as I have feelings and thoughts, I will continue to articulate them. Words express the impulses from the innermost part of my soul and become the narrative in a story or poem.

I wonder what these words would look like if they were dancing? Would they be swirling around in graceful pirouettes as I express my endless devotion to you? If my words were musical notes, would they evoke a joyful melody of harmony and love and at other times frantic, distressed, discordant sounds of anger and disbelief over your passing? If my words were a drawing would their colors, shapes, forms and gestures clearly convey to the viewer my primal motherly nature that always wanted to protect you and my subsequent powerlessness in averting your death? If my words were a rose would the lovely fragrance from its blossoms heighten one's senses from the sweet perfume of a mother's love for her child? If my words were the ocean would their magnificent expanse and unfathomable depth bring spiritual renewal and rejuvenation to one's suffering soul? If my words were a mountain, would they take one from the valley of despair, to the peak of the highest heavens? And if my words were a tree, would they bring spiritual nourishment to all the broken hearted parents that need strength and stability to go through life without their child?

These are my words. My elocution of silent speech forming into emotionally compelling shapes and symbols to represent the voice wishing to be expressed from my soul.

I love you,
Mother

I WEAR YOU

Dear Jai,

I wear you; you are my emotional attire. You're the tears in my eyes, the sigh in my breath, the heaviness in my heart. Anyone who has grieved, will see that I mourn for you; anyone who is heartbroken, will see that I long for you. I wear you; you are my emotional attire. You're the light in my eyes, the life force in my breath, the joy in my heart, the laughter in my voice. My garb is the coexistence of opposites. They fit me quite well as I journey through the grieving process of your young demise. The most beautiful ensemble I wear is this chain of love: the infinite thread that links our souls for all eternity.

Jai, I wear you, you are my heavenly attire.

Love,
Mother

YOUR LIFE CYCLE

Dear Jai,

December 10, 2019

You were the embryo in my womb that grew into a fetus,
that formed into a baby,
that sprouted into a toddler,
that blossomed into a young boy,
that developed into a teenager,
that matured into a man.
That was the end of your cycle:
your life was completed.

Love you,
Mom

A BEAUTIFUL LIFE

Dear Jai,

December 12, 2019

Your love is the breath we breathe. Each moment of every day is a moment of loving you: the joy in our hearts. We honor the great man that you were: a beautiful life that once was. We pay homage to our dear, wonderful:
son
brother
godson
nephew
cousin
grandchild
boyfriend
friend
business partner
Grieving you is loving you:
opposite sides of the same coin.

Your essence,
your soul,
your divinity,
is always alive
and with us.

Love is the silent voice that unifies our hearts.*
Love is the eternal thread that links our souls.
Love is the sacred place where we hold our

dear, Justin, Jai.

Love,
Mother

* The poem inscribed on the memorial plaque.

THE CEILING

Dear Justin,

December 12, 2019

The ceiling has been blown wide open, no more concealing my feelings of sadness for you my dear Jai. Anywhere and everywhere the raw, open wound of grieving your loss is exposed. Actually quite liberating, no more hiding my emotions.

My tears flow unobstructed, opening me up and moving out the tension that is locked up inside me. Salty waters, like that of the great oceans, wash through every part of me and I feel cleansed.

Justin, everything is a reminder of you: losses, gains, new beginnings, and endings. Your absence during these events is a painful reminder that you're gone from this world. Activities that I am involved in no longer have you as a part of them to share with. In these moments I profoundly feel your physical absence and the striking reality of your passing is experienced all over again. This is when my tears show up. They are good. They are not something that is harmful or need to be overcome. It doesn't mean that I am not doing well with my grieving process, on the contrary. For me it's an expression of my unending love for you and you are worth every tear that I shed. My tears are a natural by-product of my broken heart. My love flows out to humanity and joins other mothers' tears in the great unbounded ocean of love for our deceased children. We keep our children's memories, our sacred treasures, close to us like priceless, precious gems.

All is well as I voyage through a most liberating journey in this life of mine.

Loving you always,
Mom

DYING

Dear Jai,

December 14, 2019

What was it like to die, to shed your skin and no longer wear your body? That complex, amazing physiology reflecting God's brilliant intelligence and genius creation.

Did your soul along with your last breath move out of your body at the speed of light and exit through the crown of your head?

How did it feel to no longer have in your peripheral vision your body with its edges and lines to determine the boundaries around you? All of a sudden you are free of the dense carcass you had all your life, and no longer have the physical limitations you grew accustomed to holding you back. That must have been quite a phenomenal experience to get used to.

Did you feel totally embraced by love? Were you full of only light now that there was no more density to conceal it? Did you meet up with your great grandparents, grandparents, and Aunts Denise and Colleen? Was my higher Soul Self there to greet you? Were there divine facilitators guiding and loving you so you could acclimate to this new and sudden reality with comfort and ease? Did you visit all the different realms in creation? Are you learning about the mysteries of the universe? Did you feel my extreme sorrow and motherly love when I received the news that you died?

Did you see your mother absolutely distraught and in all my human frailty screaming and banging my fists on the dashboard of the car when the doctor told dad and I you were dead?

Justin, please tell me is there an art to dying? Justin, please tell me about life and death. Justin, please tell me about heaven.

Loving you for all eternity my dear son,
Mom

TUNNEL OF BLISS

Dear Jai,

December 15, 2019

When I was in my 20's I had an extremely powerful experience. I woke up in the middle of the night to find my awareness moving through a tunnel. I shot through this long narrow structure at the speed of sound. I heard a loud humming as I zoomed through it with intense velocity. The speed at which I was moving seem to be making this sound. At the same time, bliss ran throughout my physiology, incredibly strong and overpowering my small human body. It was like nothing I have ever known before or since.

My whole being was rapidly moving in an upward motion and a magnetic pull of bliss was surging inside of me. I suddenly realized, "If I continue on like this, I am going to leave my body." I immediately fell back to sleep the second I had the thought, and woke up the next morning.

In the years following this amazing moment, I started to hear about near-death experiences and people's claim of going through a tunnel to the light. Sounded like what happened to me, but I didn't get to the light.

I was a young, healthy woman. I wasn't dying and I didn't have an accident. I was supposed to be asleep in bed, and yet I was going through this tunnel, but why?

Physicist Albert Einstein theorized that space and time are not a separate or unrelated phenomena, but actually interlaced into a single continuum called space-time that spans multiple dimensions.

Was my consciousness spanning through the numerous dimensions of space-time?

Was I bridging many realities all at once?

Was my 25-year-old self having a moment of 41 years into the future: the sudden death of my son and his blissful entry into the light?

Jai, was I actually being given a glimpse of your tunnel experience on the day you died?

Is this what transcending the boundaries of space-time means, an intricate weaving of past, present and future happening simultaneously?

Having a peek at what you might have experienced going through the tunnel brings me solace.

As complex as this whole reality of multidimensionality is, your mother is comforted that you were in a blissful state of being.

Loving you forever,
Mom

BEGINNINGS AND ENDINGS

Dear Jai,

December 19, 2019

Each day is a new beginning, A point in space and time when something is born again. The birth of another sunrise, another rainbow, another snowfall. In this endless continuum of infinity, we use a point in our three-dimensional world to mark the beginning of seasons, holidays and new years.

Your 32nd birthday was the beginning of celebrating your special day without you.

This Thanksgiving and Christmas is the beginning of not having you in our lives anymore to share the festivities.

These beginnings are deeply interwoven into endings, and the ending of your earthly life as a human being. I do believe you live in spirit and your essence lives on within me, but your human incarnation is over. That ending was the beginning of a void, a gap in the space between the end of your dynamic earthly life and the beginning of your heavenly existence.

Your ending created the beginning of a new life for you; a new form, back to the formless expression that you were before you took on your notable, human appearance.

Beginnings and endings are really an illusion. We are the ones that mark the boundaries from start to finish, to create an orderly sequence in the events of life, and through it all the infinite stream of our love moves forward transcending this illusion we call time.

Loving you so deeply,
Mother

TAPESTRY OF YOUR LIFE

Dear Jai,

December 20, 2019

The design of your life was built upon a sequential unfoldment of events. Like a beautiful tapestry of threads woven together: to create the parts of the whole of who you were to be. All the weavings of your individuality from one stitch to the next created the unique human being with the identity of, Justin 'Jai' Malloy. You came from the formless and from your inception grew into a handsome creation recognized as a young man.

You fashioned your life around goodness, fun, love, authenticity, creativity, happiness and passion.

These are the threads that your consciousness found expression through and a magnificent embroidery was crafted from a dynamic life well lived.

Loving your creation.

Always,
Mom

LOSS

Dear Jai,

December 21, 2019

A big jolt of an uncomfortable reality has hit me hard. I see how events can take place so suddenly and life can turn out quite differently from the vision I had in my head.

Since I have experienced the worst that can happen to a mother, which was losing my child, I've lost my innocence. Trusting that all will be fine in the future seems like a naive way to live, and can lead to future disappointments.

I feel it's time for me to grow up, and be a realistic adult. I know that life can knock me down again and again, because it has, but I'm still standing and will continue to move forward. Eventually I will find peace in my present circumstances.

Living in the present without any expectations is how I like to live life now. Being in the moment feels safer. Appreciating what is right now, is the only place I wish to be.

Love,
Mom

LAST CHRISTMAS

Dear Jai,

Last Christmas, 2018, you brought your girlfriend, Angelique, home to Iowa to celebrate the holiday season with your family. You met her at your friend's wedding party and was immediately smitten. There was a sweet chemistry between the two of you: playful, kind, spiritual, and you both liked to laugh together. I enjoyed seeing you content and happy with this young woman. At 31 years old you found love. Our family of four was beginning to expand with the addition of your significant other being brought into the family fold.

I'm remembering sitting on the couch on a cold December morning. The warmth from the fireplace was taking the chill out of the living room. A 14-foot-tall Douglas fir tree adorned the space with numerous ornaments: sparkly glass painted balls, a framed baby photo of you, Santa Claus in all shapes and sizes, pretty angels and gold garland wrapped around the tree in a big holiday hug.

You were busy opening up your presents: shirts in your favorite colors of blue and black, a cotton gray sweatsuit, a pair of earbuds, and of course packages of new underwear and socks. A friend made a piece of wall art we purchased for your home. It was a rectangular shaped frame with live wild grasses mounted on top of a green wallpaper background enclosed in glass. You admired the organic nature of this style of art and the artist's creativity.

We had a wonderful time together.

It was the last Christmas we would celebrate with you. The

following summer you were destined to have a tragic accident and suddenly die.

A parents' worst nightmare.

On, June 29, 2019, the day before you passed away, we had our final telephone conversation. You called home to say hi to dad and I. As we were about to say good-bye I suggested that the family come to you in Sacramento for our next Christmas celebration. You said it was a great idea. We then said, "I love you'" and hung up.

This Christmas Angelique is in deep mourning. After you died she moved back to New Mexico to live with her parents and heal from the shock. She was 24 years old and your death was intensely traumatic for her. Your sister doesn't want to come home for the holiday since your absence will be too much for her to bear. Her heart is shattered.

I decided that dad and I should still come to the West coast for Christmas even though you are no longer there. This trip will be a pilgrimage for us to the land you loved, and we will spend time with family and many of your friends who are deeply grieving you.

We will start out at Aunt Sharon's house in Napa Valley and wind our way down through the magnificent vineyards of wine country to Santa Cruz. Once we arrive we will stay with your dear friends, Pete, Shea and their sweet pup, Kiki. We will then go and have a delicious dinner at your good buddy Eric's home that is tucked away in the woods of Bonny Doon. Many of your friends will gather there as a way to honor you and your parents' visit.

This trip will be our way to pay tribute to your life and observe our final conversation of coming to California for the holiday, now you will be with us in spirit only.

Love you,
Mom

FIRST CHRISTMAS

My dear Jai,

December 23, 2019

This is my first Christmas since you passed away. My years of excitement of baking your favorite holiday foods, preparing your bedroom for your arrival, decorating the house with all the splendor of the season, and buying you gifts, has come to an abrupt halt. It's interesting how an activity that has been so ingrained in me all of my life and brought so much happiness has lost its joy this year.

As I walk along the shopping mall, looking at the displays in the windows, my mind is suddenly drawn to the holiday songs playing over the loud speaker.

I start to tear up.

I hear a song about the pending birth of baby, Jesus, and his blessed mother, Mary, and I know someday she will lose her child in an awful crucifixion. Her son is going to die at around the same age you died.

The sympathy I have always felt for Mary and the violent death she as a mother had to witness as her beautiful son was being crucified has taken on an even deeper meaning for me.

My sympathy has turned into empathy for another mother's loss because as mothers we are all connected in our maternal hearts. In the universal ocean of a mother's love for her child, we are all one and no matter who we are, our losses powerfully unify us.

Always loving you, my dear Jai,
Mother

DEEP SIGHS

Dear Jai,

December 23, 2019

I am thinking about your passing and my heart feels waves of sadness washing over it along with deep sighs, a precursor to the flood of tears that follow when the impact of your sudden demise hits me again, and again and again.

My sighs come in those moments of frustration that I, in some miraculous way could have prevented your death. As unreasonable as it may seem it's only natural for a mother to always want to protect her child, no matter how old the child.

My sighs are deep breaths, inhaling and exhaling as I think of you and the overpowering love I feel for you, my dear son.

It's plain and simple, I don't like you being dead!!!

I look at your photo and my mind tells me you were only meant to live a short life. I know that, it's obvious, but it doesn't stop the pain I feel. At times my body feels empty, flat, other times the heaviness of grief sits on me and I feel too weak to move.

I try to accept this reality with all the spiritual jargon I have heard over the years and feel it's time to put it to good use. Bottom line is, even with my understanding that we all come to this world with a soul contract, and we have a certain number of breaths. I still can't bear it you are no longer with me in human form. I'm not going to make a mood and act like I don't feel this way or I need to stop grieving because it may make you unhappy on the other side.

I don't believe that.

I will continue mourning you and go through the process a mother goes through that has lost her dear child. Time will change the experience of grief and my surrender to what is will become more acceptable.

I will move on with a sense of loss and love and never forget you, but I will sigh as I think of all that has been lost.

Loving and sighing so deeply when I think of you,
Mother

THIS CHRISTMAS

My dear Jai,

December 25, 2019

We just arrived here in California. Your father and I want to acknowledge my last conversation with you about coming to see you for Christmas.

Your dad became upset when we flew into the San Francisco airport. Memories of you picking him up for your father/son vacations, brought back special moments in his life with you. He was thinking about your trip to Catalina Island. You were both having a great time cruising around the streets in a golf cart with the sunshine beating down on your tanned bodies. The expansiveness of the ocean and the different vantage points you could view it from was awe inspiring. The Spanish style architecture of the arboretum was charming, and dad took a fabulous photo of you standing in the portico with the ocean in the distance. All these images of your past together conjured up much sadness in your father.

Being here without you has given me a sense of closure. I was surprised to experience this and had no idea I even needed it, but on some level, I did. Coming to where you lived, and not finding you here anymore, was another layer of the reality that you had left. You lived in California for the past thirteen years and not seeing you at the airport, curbside pick-up to greet us, verged on the feeling of abandonment. My limbs went numb.

This realization that your human incarnation is permanently over has kept my grief in check. My daily bouts of profuse tears are taking a much-needed rest and instead, they're sitting deep inside my broken heart, and being quiet for now.

Something I've learned about myself since you died is that I need to face things head on and look them right in the eye. There is no stuffing of feelings for this Italian Mamma. That is why journaling to you and probing deeply into your life, past, present and after life, has been a good process for me. It puts life and its events into a broader perspective. I gain a deeper understanding that is helpful to a degree, but in no way cancels out how much I miss you, and the constant ache I feel in my heart. The spark of the divine is what animates me as a human and allows me to feel sadness, love, joy and everything else that is part of my humanity. It's a gift that can deeply hurt as well.

Dad and I will walk the path of our past visits with you and see your friends, family, place of work, and favorite restaurants. We will go to West Cliff and breathe in the salty ocean air and think of you with deep love and reverence.

We feel much gratitude for the time we did have together and the moments we shared.

Always loving you,
Mom

MY WORDS-MY PRAYERS

Dear Jai,

December 26, 2019

My words line up as continuous prayers around you,
They dance along as expressions of love and adoration for you,
They are the fingers on my prayer beads of endless requests to you,
They are the fine threads of feelings I have about you.

Love,
Mom

MY LOVE FOR YOU

Dear Justin,

December 26, 2019

My love for you cannot be left behind. It has influenced all areas of my life and my interactions with; family, friends, acquaintances, strangers and the world. My love for you has activated a rapport within myself to better understand humanity. The light in you is now appreciated as the light in others. My love for you is a gift that allows me to navigate through the eternal and timeless journey of knowing our divinity, immortality and God Self. My love for you is my practice, my program, my meditation, to transcend through the finest feelings until I arrive at the source of my Being. My love for you is my prayer to the Divine presence for greater depth of understanding, to eventually break through this veil of sadness and find our souls united in the deep recesses of my heart. My love for you has given me the emotional elasticity to experience the depths of my grief to the heights of my joy.

My love for you is infinite and eternal.

Love,
Mom

PILGRIMAGE OF HONORING

Dear Justin,

December 29, 2019

For the last four days I've been on a pilgrimage of honoring your life: visiting your friends in California and the special spots we frequented with you while you were still alive. This is my Christmas tribute to you. Tracing the steps back to your life in Sacramento and Santa Cruz is giving me a strong sense of the finality of your life, but your spirit, Jai, feels quite lively. Your presence is felt everywhere: I feel you in your friends, in the love and warmth they exude. I see you in their eyes, and the familiar light shining through. I hear you in their laughter, in your similar sense of humor. I know you in their youthfulness, with the vitality and strength you had.

The stories they tell me about their time with you are heartwarming; the way you brought people together, the confidence you had in your business affairs, your generous heart, and the way you helped friends that were struggling with relationships,

Dad and I met a new friend of yours for dinner. He heard we were coming to town and wanted to meet your parents. He told us he was going through a divorce. He loved his wife, but she was unfaithful to him. He was crushed. He said you stood by him during this difficult time, giving him your sage advice. He was impressed with your warm and caring nature; your friendship meant a lot to him.

Feeling all this love from your friends is a healing balm for my broken heart.

You loved living in California. There was a fullness of life that you experienced there. You were deeply loved, honored and respected by all who knew you. This is where you grew into your manhood. This is where your success was waiting for you.

As I walk the path of your life and get a glimpse of your years on the West Coast, I feel happy; my heart is nourished and soothed.

Our divine connection is strengthening as I review the different phases of your life and reflect on your eventual passing.

Loving your forever,
Mom

NEW YEAR 2020

Dear Jai,

So this is the New Year and how does it feel?
To have you away, it seems so surreal.

A Happy New Year, it isn't there yet;
I live each and every day and have no regret.

Another year ending and what have I done?
I mourned my womanhood and then grieved my son.

A very Merry Christmas was not to be had,
I miss you so deeply and so does your Dad.

Please give me some guidance on how to get through,
a lifetime no longer of living with you.

Through all the festivities and happy good cheer,
I now must admit I did feel you near.

Shining your light from wherever you are,
you opened by heart; you didn't feel far.

At the end of my life when it's all said and done,
I'll say to myself, "I had a good run."

Loving you forever,
Mom

EMOTIONAL DAM

Dear Jai,

January 2, 2020

The new year has come on with a big emotional wallop. It's difficult going through the holidays and a new calendar year without you being in it. You didn't live to 2020.

I had a major melt down before. I looked at your photo and suddenly became a raging, angry mother, railing against every spiritual being and belief I have. It triggered something in me and my emotional dam broke. All this pent-up rage erupted out of me.

I screamed like a crazy person. I stamped my feet like an angry child and said to God, "I don't accept this!" I have no idea what good this does, if any, but it's my personal battle with reality.

I'm exhausted, my throat hurts from yelling so long, hard and deep. I need to take a rest.

Missing you

Love,
Mother

HEARTS OF LIGHT

Dear Jai,

January 3, 2020

Exactly one month before you passed away I sent you a text. It was a photo of two hearts of light that appear every morning on my bedroom ceiling between 7:30-8:30 a.m. After I sent you the photos, I texted, "I'm sending you all the love these hearts represent" and I wished you a beautiful day. You exclaimed; "Amazing!"

I had a very heavy day of grieving yesterday. That evening I was watching television in the family room. All of a sudden, I noticed a heart of light suspended in mid-air at the top of the ceiling. It was purely celestial and had nothing to do with any outside light reflecting onto the ceiling since it was dark out.

What I realized, my dear sweet son, is that you were sending back to me a heart of heavenly light. I felt still and complete inside myself as I was witnessing this vision of love from you.

Loving you from my heart of light to yours.

Always,
Mother

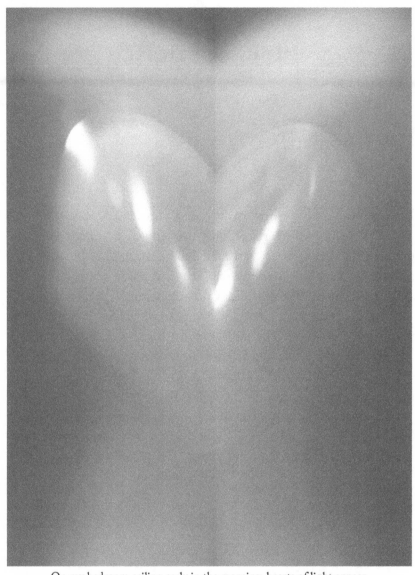

On my bedroom ceiling early in the morning, hearts of light appear.

GRACEFULLY NAVIGATE

Dear Jai,

January 5, 2020

Mourning you is my way of honoring you. In the first year of your passing the loss still feels fresh and new: a deep open wound needing time to heal. Along with grieving you are the day-to-day subtleties that this new reality encompasses. The various aspects of life that have been affected now that you are no longer in human form.

For instance, how do I respond to people I meet for the first time when they ask me if I have any children without falling apart when I answer them? Do I say I have a daughter and son and leave out that you died, if it's not an appropriate time to get into that detail?

Visiting California over the Christmas season and not seeing you there, especially when we went to your work place, was another painful confirmation that you died. You weren't there to give us a tour of the greenhouses and update us on the latest technology in plant propagation. The place felt empty without your presence, a building that lost its soul.

Then what to do with the storage unit where a lot of your possessions are sitting and waiting for a new home? It feels so creepy and cold to have your things sitting in there. Like a dark spooky morgue where your belongings are in a holding pattern, waiting for a new owner to give them a useful purpose.

The list goes on. There's a lot to get used to. I do believe in time I will learn how to gracefully navigate through this life without you in it.

One thing I know for sure, as life goes on, my love for you will outweigh my grief.

Loving you always,
Mom

HOLY MOMENT

Dear Jai,

January 6, 2020

The last day we spoke on the phone was the day before you passed away. Little did I know it would be the last time I would say hello to you, and how crucial our good-bye would be. Do we ever know the depth of each moment we are living and the impact it has on the future? Or how prophetic the words that we say to one another, words like good-bye can mean something so final?

Once the understanding of that place in time came to pass, our phone conversation took on a whole new meaning and will stay with me for the rest of my life. It dawned on me, that day was a holy moment in space and time: hidden within it a rite of passage.

The stage was set marking our farewell to one another, the significance of our conversation became a spiritual event for us. We spoke to each other for the last time before your death that would take place in less than 24 hours. The end of your life on earth was imminent. Our good-bye was a transitional point for your upcoming entrance into the celestial field.

What a hallowed, landmark instant we shared.

Dear Justin, I am loving you beyond the confines of space and time and cherishing every word and moment we've had together.

Love,
Mom

EACH DAY

Dear Justin,

Each day you are gone from my world is another day of living without you. I wonder what the day will look like as I watch it wake up from the sleepy nighttime pause, and enters into the daily nuances of living life.

What will trigger my tears of sorrow for your loss today? How will I reconcile my tears and what will I move onto next?

Every moment in my life is different since you died, and nothing will ever feel the same without you being here.

I wake up in the middle of the night with the full moon shining into my bedroom windows. It feels like it's 6 a.m. when it's really only 3. I'm wide awake and take this opportunity to get up and write to you and so I do. In these quiet moments when everything is asleep, I take the time to feel into what I want to say without any of the daytime distractions getting in the way.

I feel you in the silence, it's just the two of us, one to one. I wonder how your journey is coming along. I wonder how you feel about how I am coping with your death and if you have any advice to offer me.

I feel you between the veil, transparent and unseen. You feel huge, as though you are everywhere at the same time, and yet the personality of Justin is still present so I can recognize you.

I love you,
Mom

DOUBLE WHAMMY

My dear love,

January 10, 2020

My chest aches, and at times it's hard to know if it's from the double mastectomy or the deep ache in my heart over losing you. Then I realize, they are one and the same. The loss of what my breasts represent to my womanhood, the soft and nurturing part of my motherhood; these physical appendages have now been removed from my life and so have you.

Looking back, the mastectomy surgery appeared as an omen of what was to come four months later: your death. Very interesting how everything coincided. The karmic postman was after me.

My emotional, spiritual, physical, and mental equilibrium have been thrown off and I am working my way back to finding my center. It will be a different center from where I was before all of these events. How can it not be?

I am not who I once was and neither are you. I never thought I would be looking back on your life as something from the past that no longer exists. Now that you are gone it is what I do each and every day.

Resting, meditating, exercising, eating balanced organic meals, writing, spending time with loved ones, are all rebuilding my life, a life which you are no longer a physical part of.

My love for you, dear one, has grown exponentially. This rapid growth has accelerated not only my motherly feelings of love for you, but also my love for all of life. I now encompass a broader understanding of what being human means. I feel myself as a part of everything as I move through the multiple changes taking place in my reality.

You have expanded me, and I thank you.

I love you,
Mom

SERENITY PRAYER

Dear Jai,

I woke up again not being able to sleep through the night. There's a powerful full moon that is lasting for three days. It's called the, "Super Blood Wolf Moon." This is a rare event where the moon appears bigger and brighter than usual.

I went into the T.V. room to watch a little television and see if I could fall asleep in there. I woke up an hour later to the sound of three distinct female voices reciting in unison the famous Serenity Prayer:

"God grant me the serenity to accept the things I can not change, the courage to change the things I can, and the wisdom to know the difference."

By Reinhold Niebuhr

At first I thought it was coming from the T.V., but it wasn't... It became clear that the voices and the invocation they were reciting was a message from you and the angels.

As I journey through this life without you, I will think of this petition and the sweet voices reciting it, and it will bring me much needed consolation and strength.

Thank-you, the angels and of course Reinhold for this divine prayer.

Love,
Mom

147

SONG OF LOVE

Dear Justin,

January 15, 2020

As I reflect upon the events of your life,
I observe the unfolding of a divine composition.
You were playing your solo act as Justin,
along with the orchestration of your
family and friends to lend their
love and support, as you navigated your way
through this existence.
Your chose a fast tempo to move through the
short time you would have here.
Your soul knew it would be a quick beat,
so an outpouring of lovely melodies joined
together to convey your story.

You had your own unique collaboration with God
on how to sing your song.
The song of your life was a song of love, in the key
of harmony and happiness.

Always singing your praises,
Mom

TIME

Dear Jai,

January 18, 2020

Your life didn't appear to be done, but according to the cosmic plan that no one was aware of, it ended. You were quietly moving forward on your own trajectory towards the moment of your sudden passing.

Everyone's life plays out within a span of activity as they sojourn on Earth. Every moment, year, and cycle moves through this configuration we call time.

There are periods when the junction point of events seem perfect and the alignment of circumstances appear to be magical. A lot of your life seemed to be that way, plus you worked very hard to make it happen. Meeting the love of your life, having a great team of investors and scientists for your business, living in the natural beauty on the West Coast, and making so many amazing friends, who were like family to you.

Then there are those times when everything seems off. Nothing appears to align or make any sense to the human mind or the way the mind likes to construct how things should be, especially when something tragic happens. Your death appears to be one of those instances that doesn't line up: personally, karmically, dharmically or however else I want to judge it.

As far as where you were in time and everything you were working towards, your death just didn't make sense. That's what my mind likes to tell me as I look at the surface value of who you were.

I also believe there are no accidents in the universe especially in the destiny of one's own death. You were an incredibly dynamic person, in tip top shape. You were committed to keeping a good routine and self-care. There was a higher power acting out that trumped all your efforts to live a long life.

Who am I to judge what should and shouldn't be, or when one should live or die? Of course, I know how I want life to be, but that is not necessarily how it may turn out. At this point in the world we live in, it's very harsh at times.

Your soul was on its own personal time line, traveling to the beat of Justin.

So, my dear son, as I put the events of your life under the microscope of my probing mind, and the images of who you were upon it, it appears that you didn't have time to get everything done, but I now see that life gets done on its own time.

Love,
Mom

DISASSEMBLE

Dear Jai,

January 20, 2020

Yesterday your Dad told me he is planning on disassembling our pool table and donating it to the Student Union Center at our local university.

I thought about the word "disassemble" and how it related to your death and the impact it had on Dad.

Father and son would come together to bond over a game of pool and catch up on life. Beginning in your teen years and continuing into adulthood and holiday visits home, you both looked forward to spending time together playing pool.

Simultaneously the sports images flashed on the T.V. screen, while the two of you got your competitive juices flowing. A lighthearted competition would erupt, with loud exclamations of oohs and aahs in expressions of defeat or victory.

Now that you are gone this space is a reminder of the empty void he feels from your death. He doesn't play pool anymore. He will spend the day disassembling the table so it can be easily carried up the stairs and transported over to the university and reassembled there.

Like the dismantling of the pool table, when you died all the atoms that your body was composed of moved into a different form, into another use elsewhere in creation. Perhaps they're in a tree, another human being, or have incarnated into a brilliant star on a faraway galaxy. Your atomic structure, the subtlest part of your physical make-up, is no longer a part of you. All the parts of your life, all the dreams you had and Dad had for you, have

151

been permanently disassembled. You played your final game and instead have been fully reassembled into a being of light.

Your absence and the realization of what the pool table represents to your father is weighing heavy on his heart today.

Love,
Mom

GRIEF NERVE

My dear Jai,

January 25, 2020

I'm continuing to experience trigger point moments that activate my grief nerve. Hearing the sounds of an ambulance screaming by me on the road, can stimulate a bout of deep sadness and many tears. I recognize that is the same sound in the environment the day you drowned. Medics were on their way in the ambulance, running their sirens and hoping to get to you in time to save your life.

In this trigger point moment, I realize that in the present time, I'm hearing another place in time and it's, Yours. The urgency of the sirens and the life-threatening situation these sounds communicate to me, elicit that tragic event in my memory all over again.

I had a vision three years ago. I sat down to meditate and I saw an ambulance stopped on a wide street with their red lights flashing. It was a clear sunny day, somewhere, someplace, U.S.A. There was no other information with the image before me. It came to me numerous times over the course of several months. It was so real, but I didn't know what it was trying to tell me. Obviously, there was a pressing situation that I was witnessing in my mind's eye.

Now I do know.

When Dad and I went to your house the day after you passed, I noticed it was on a wide avenue across from a school: the same street I saw in my vision.

Perhaps these images and internal prodding's are from a higher source of my inner knowingness. Are they there to help me deal with unpleasant situations when they do eventually occur?

This seems to be a theme in my life, glimpsing an event before it happens, gives me a heads up without knowing the sad details, protecting my emotions. I would hate to live with the cognizance for several years that you were going to die. All I can do is silently watch what is being shown on my screen of consciousness and let destiny unfold.

It's all in God's hands.

Always loving you,
Mom

SURRENDER

Dear Jai,

January 25, 2020

I'm beginning to see how grief has taught me how to surrender. What appears to be the most inconvenient moment for me to have a grief meltdown, seems to be the time when sadness comes over me. To feel so vulnerable, raw and exposed at any moment is an act in letting go. Grief doesn't necessarily live by the social norms of when a certain behavior is acceptable. Having lunch with friends, at a birthday party, family gathering, can be an invitation for the floodgates to open.

At the most inopportune times, something will spark a memory of you and your presence becomes enlivened in my awareness. I feel a wave of your spirit washing through me. In this moment I have no choice but to go with it. Surrender is a way of yielding my emotional control and allows me to honor you.

I surrender to loving you always.

Love,
Mother

AND SO IT GOES

Dear Jai,

January 26, 2020

It's early Sunday morning. I'm sitting alone thinking about you. You come to the forefront of my mind, since I had previously lost you in the background haze of the night time slumber. Like a loyal friend, you resurface in the quiet dawn of a new day. I feel sad and shed my tears, my endless tears over your passing. Your presence comes on so strong. You feel alive and right here with me. Your soft and kind manner is palpable, sitting with me in my silence. I revel in experiencing you. You have come back to me and my tears continue to flow.

The moment eventually passes, my tears subside and so it goes.

Always loving your memory,
Mom

THE NATION MOURNS KOBE BRYANT
AND HIS DAUGHTER, GIANNA

Dear Jai,

January 26, 2020

News of loss. Loved ones and public figures abruptly leaving this earth without any warning; leaving us in shock. How do we move forward? We can end up drowning in tears of sorrow or keep treading water to prevent us from fully submerging into the sea of grief.

Every moment of everyday a loss happens. Today we lost a beloved sports figure and his young daughter in a tragic accident, and a whole nation mourns together.

Humanity is unified in the experience of a national heartache. The burden is shared by many and the weight of the misfortune may feel slightly lighter as we weather the storm.

All blessings to Kobe Bryant and his precious daughter, Gianna. I pray for strength for his dear wife and children.

Love you,
Mom

THE JUSTIN BUTTON

Dear Jai,

January 28, 2020

I have your voice message on my cell phone. I taped it off the landline of the call you made to Dad and I the day before you passed away.

That Saturday, I came into the kitchen and heard you leaving a message for us and so I immediately picked up the phone. The three seconds of the message you were leaving is a gift. I love hearing your soft, sweet voice saying "hi" and that you were thinking of your parents. Thank you! I'm also glad I managed to get to the phone in time to speak to you. That was another gift from you.

Right now, I'm looking at the memo on my cell phone and my finger wants to press down on the button and play the message, but I decide not to. I assess the moment and realize this is not a good time for me to have a potential melt down, even though I would I love to hear your voice. I exert some self-control and decide not to press the Justin button right now.

Another day, at another time I will, but just not now.

Loving you so much,
Mother

FROM HUMAN BEING TO CELESTIAL BEING

Dear Jai,

January 30, 2020

I realize that my grief is based on missing you and your human beingness, which is no more. Our communication is no longer between two humans. You changed into a celestial heavenly creature and I am still a dense, earth-bound person.

The reality of this feels distant and unfamiliar to me, since I have known you for 31 years as Justin "Jai" and that is how I was used to relating to you. I realize the person you once were no longer exists. Your body's ashes have been given back to Mother Earth.

The vision I had in my head of how I thought life would turn out for you, is now an illusion. A new reality is in order and I must abide by it. My prayer to you, my dear son, is that in time I can let go my deep attachment of who you were and how we related with each other.

This is a challenging journey I am on. I'm trying to look at the grieving process from all sides, and asking for your help in allowing me to rise up and live the most enlightened perspective.

I need to move with grace and ease into the new status of who you have transformed into.

Loving you always,
Mother

YOU ROSE ABOVE ME

Dear Jai,

January 31, 2020

You rose above me,
as my tears keep pouring down around me.

I don't recognize you,
my heart is in pieces,
as I try to put you back together within it;
the place where your new identity resides.
Please see me,
stand with me and walk by my side,
while we journey through our new reality together.
I listen for you to call my name
in quiet whispers as our subtle
conversations open me up to
deep reflections of who we have become.

You rose above me as my tears keep
pouring down around me.

Love,
Mom

OH LIFE!

Dear Jai,

Oh life!

Jai, it's been eight months since you left us, since you went back home to heaven.

I feel sad without you. Tears keep falling; I can't resist them. The pain is sharp and deep. Nothing takes your place.

I'm out of faith, just believing in the moment it's all that's real ... if that.

Fortune tellers were wrong. I'm living a reality I'm not familiar with. Time to change the mindset. The old vision is now a fantasy.

Oh life!

I need to keep my eye on you. I'm being led one way, and finding you the other.

What's the new plan? Let's think about it, meditate on it, sing about it.

I'm swallowing my pride as my eyes are opening wide.

Oh life!

Loving you,
Mother

EVERLASTING LOVE

Dear Jai,

February 1, 2020

You left when I needed you most.
So you gave me your everlasting love.
You came into my life to complete my circle.
You gave me some of your time and all your sweetness.
I couldn't have lived without it.
You were my baby boy.
I held you when you slept.
I hugged you when you wept.
A beautiful young man you would become.
A son second to none.
You left when I needed you most.
So you gave me your everlasting love.

Eternally yours,
Mom

GOOD-BYE AND HELLO

Dear Jai,

February 1, 2020

I forget myself,
perhaps you need to remind me,
who am I to be?
It has been evading me.
Can you help find me?
I look around and your
absence is in my face,
always in my face,
always a heartache around every corner.
Nothing is forever, except our love,
for now though, it's good-bye.
Someday in another universe it will be hello again.

I love you,
Mother

THE PLAN

Dear Jai,

You were just beginning,
the plan was in your hands,
but it was already written,
your life would be ending,
and in the silence you left us.
The plan was in God's hands,
it was already written and off
you went.

Loving you always,
Mother

DROPS OF HEAVEN

Dear Jai,

February 2, 2020

Drops of heaven sprinkling around me;
glitters of blue and you descend upon me.
In quiet solitude you embrace me;
I feel your stillness envelope me.
I'm looking for you out there,
but you're no longer in my atmosphere.
Is heaven everything you hoped it would be?
Did you find yourself climbing a golden tree?
And when you touch down once again,
please say hello to me, your mother, your friend.

Loving you always,
Mom

THIS HEART

Dear Jai,

This heart of mine will never stop loving you.
It will never stop beating for you;
this heart of mine is always breathing you.

I close my eyes; you stand before me.
I open my eyes; you rise above me.

Your stillness envelopes me.

I'm sure there's so much more to tell me,
so much more that we can say.

My awareness dives into the
crystal-clear fibers of your being,
shimmering radiance sparkling on the edges of my life.
Your light is seen in shades of blue,
bottomless joy taking me into the ocean of your bliss,
waves of love come crashing into my heart.

This heart of mine will never stop loving you.
It will never stop beating for you;
this heart of mine is always breathing you.

Love,
Mom

I CARRY ON

Dear Jai,

Even though you went away,
your love remains, you left behind the
best part of you; your essence
is pulsating throughout me.

The delicate fibers of your heart are
interwoven into mine.
I carry on wearing the finery of your love
with great pride and dignity.

How do I thank you for coming into my life,
if only for a short while?
Paying tribute to a life well lived,
respecting the memory of the great
man you were, and the divine being you
have become.

Even though you went away, my heart
overflows with love for you each and every day.

Flowing with love,
Mom

SO MUCH TO SAY

Dear Jai,

February 5, 2020

There's so much I want to tell you,
so much I need to say.
I look around me, but you have gone away.

You have touched my soul
down deep inside; my
feelings are unleashed,
there's nothing left to hide.

Feelings of love pierce through this
heavy veil,
prayers lining up telling God my sad tale.
A story about a young man who suddenly
went away and his grieving mother
who was left in much dismay.

Into adulthood you would grow;
we really didn't know that would be the
end of your show.

As you were heading towards the
heavenly light,
the presence of Divine Mother
was always in your sight.

There's so much I want to tell you,
so much I wish to say.

I look around me, but you have gone away.

Love,
Mom

YOUR LOVE

Dear Jai,

February 8, 2020

Your love illuminates the words on the page;
open up the door and let them take center stage.

From the depths of silence is where they emerge,
about your life and you were on the verge;
moving into the phase of love, success, and power
and then came that fateful hour.

In a flash it came to an end.
Now all I do is send, send, send:
mountains of love and oceans of bliss,
because it's you I deeply, deeply miss.

Love,
Mother

FEELING BAD

Dear Jai,

February 9, 2020

I absolutely can't stand it that you died. How suddenly it all happened bothers the shit out of me. I am so MAD! I am incredibly SAD! I feel very BAD!

At times I can't help but feel I must have been neglectful in some way and that I could have prevented this tragic event. If only this and if only that and the yearning goes on and on. This feeling has hit me pretty hard and heavy this past weekend. Heavy gloom is sitting on me. Crying in the car as I'm driving to the store and it all come tumbling down. It's been eight months since you left us, and the grieving process seems to show up just when I think I have turned a corner, only to find it in my face all over again. How bizarre things seem right now.

Loving you always,
Mom

COAT OF GRAY

Dear Jai,

A coat of gray is being worn many days in a row.
I ask the weather to please change its attitude to
something yellow and bright.
The weeping willow couldn't take anymore heaviness
and its outstretched arms broke under the weight of gloom.
A solid sheet of ice lingers around and Mother Nature
has gone underground into a deep slumber, a state of
repose, to escape the frigid cold.

Like my dear Mother, sleep is my only
reprieve from the discomfort of your loss as I go
within to reflect on life without you.
This past summer, autumn and winter have all been wearing
a coat of gray since you went away.

It's been one long continuous freeze without you here.
I'm missing the warmth of your human presence and I
feel a bitter chill.

Love,
Mom

MY HEART

Dear Justin,

My heart is ancient and eternal. It holds the sacred space for you; from many lifetimes of loving you, and before and after time, it has loved you as well. My heart is the holy vessel where my God resides. In the most refined chambers is where I discover Her presence, the center where my human and divine emotions find expression.

My heart is the organ that beats every beat with love for you. Your presence is lively within it and continues to expand the subtle structures around it. Although you have gone away, this heart of mine loves you each and every day.

Loving you so very much,
Mother

PERCEIVE

Dear Jai,

February 11, 2020

Hey Jai, since you left this Earth, I bet you're cruising
around the universe.
So tell me, is it all you thought it would be?
How does it feel to finally be free?
How do you perceive me?
How do you find yourself to be?
A head full of curls and oh, so happy.
I'm glad you're in your bliss out there,
but for me at times it's too much to bear.
Your absence has left a mark on my heart,
I never thought we would be this far apart.
So tell me, do you miss the life you had,
spending time with me and Dad?

You know we're both very sad,
and at times I'm also mad.

Now that you found your new home, do you ever feel alone?
Have you met God in all Her glory?
Has She told you the cosmic story, of how we are all
one and never really leave?
It is just a mistake in how we perceive.

Loving you always,
Mother

FEELING YOU

Dear Justin,

There's a special feeling I become aware of when I feel you around me. It's a hugging presence, as though big soft arms are enveloping me. I breathe in deeply, with a full clear breath and I am rejuvenated. Through the subtle pranic life force, I feel us as one breath. I am silent and still; a beautiful sense of peace washes over me, and I want more of you.

Loving you so very much,
Mom

SPECIAL PLACES

Dear Jai,

February 12, 2020

There are moments with you I will remember all my life. The places we went to together: concerts, skate parks, pools, beaches, water slides and playgrounds; they are all etched in my memory. You've touched these various sites and precious moments with your presence; they are now sacred spots for me where a brilliant light once passed through.

Of all these special places that we shared together, where your beaming essence once graced, the most significant one is the space in my heart. Your mark is permanently inscribed upon it for all eternity and now the design of my life and love is constantly fixed in your memory.

Loving all the memories of our life,
Mom

NEED A SIGN

Dear Jai,

Lines have been crossed, boundaries no longer exist
between here and there, but can you give me a sign?
I always need to feel you near.
I want to know which way to grow; my world doesn't feel
safe when anything can go.
Why do things have to be this way? I lost all bearings of
what is right; you need to give me some insight.
You hit your end and we all fell apart; now it's time for
a brand-new start.
Living outside the lines, it's damn unnerving at times.
The safe and known is no more; it's time to walk through
another door.
Constantly calling out to my dear God, I wonder is
anyone even listening? Then I see the blue light
glistening.
How many steps do I need to take to enter God's
heart? I know that's where I will find you and see we're
not really apart.
When I get a glimpse of the eternal perfection, I find
my footing and right direction.

Loving you always,
Mother

CLOUDY MIST

Dear Jai,

February 14, 2020

In my memory is where you exist, without that you're just a cloudy mist, a shooting star that didn't last, a life that went by way too fast.

Jai love, I'm close behind you. I'm standing here next to you, and yet so far away: a deep distance of existence away.

A celebration of love and laughter, then came the broken heart disaster. Thirty-one years of life flew by; I thought you had at least a hundred more, but God allowed you to exit through the door.

Now your memory is where you exist, without that you're just a cloudy mist.

Loving you so deeply with a heavy heart on this Valentine's Day.

I miss you,
Mother

ARCHITECTURE OF YOUR LIFE

Dear Justin,

February 16, 2020

Your existence like all of humanity's is essentially an act of God and Her genius design in every person's conception, a creative collaboration that your parents shared in as well. The complexity of all the various facets came together to create your life, and a fine form was produced.

You were a timeless and unbounded soul housed in the architecture of a human body. The person known as my son Justin was born into the world. From the moment of your birth, Dad and I made sure we constructed a firm foundation for you to grow upon.

You grew and changed your manner and style with each phase of life, but always maintained your inner essence that was a reflection of purity, goodness, bliss, kindness, joy and love.

But, my dear son, what happened when the objective reality of your mortal life ended? When the structure of your physical body was no more? What then is the reality of the celestial field, the heavenly abode you have entered into? What I do believe is that it's just beyond the golden veil from here to there, yet so very far away in our respective realities.

You drew your first breath surrounded with your loved ones by your side and your last breath, alone, but with the angels there to guide you back home.

Love,
Mother

PARENTHOOD

My dear love,

Dad and I had a great responsibility and much joy in being your parents. From the time of your birth, into your childhood and adolescence we were with you and taking care of all your needs.

Everything we could give you we did. That's what parents do for their children and one of the ways we show our love and commitment to raising them. What was ours was yours: our home, cars, health care, food, a good education, whatever your needs were.

Then you became a young adult, living in California, working and taking care of your own needs. You matured into a self-sufficient young man.

When you passed away, everything that was yours became ours. The tables turned. Suddenly we were the owners of your vehicles, investments, jewelry, clothes, and furniture. Once again, we were sharing our worldly possessions like a family.

Even though you were living on your own for the last thirteen years, we were still your go to people. You weren't married with a family, so dad and I were your next of kin when you passed away. We were the custodians of your worldly belongings.

There's something about that status in the midst of my tears, which warms my heart. We maintained the relationship of sharing our possessions: the reciprocity of giving to one another our whole lives, until the end of your earthly incarnation.

The custodianship of being your parents encapsulates all the phases of your life, from birth to death. This conveys a closeness that stayed intact till the end of your time here.

I will always treasure our deep bond of love and the sharing we had with one another in life and after your death.

Always loving you,
Mom

EYES OF THE PAST

Dear Justin,

February 20,2020

Upon awakening this morning, your presence immediately fills my awareness. The night time gift of sleep is over and your passing floods my memory. Slumber meets the dawn and my temporary reprieve of feeling your loss is sitting with me once again.

I look to my day with the eyes of the past, and know I won't be seeing you in it. I can't call and have a chat with you about how you're doing or make plans for our next visit to California. I look into the future, but you're not there: a gloomy lens to see life through and a painful vision to carry around.

A part of myself has been thrown off course since your life ended. All your dreams, hopes and aspirations are no longer navigating the future of your destiny or acting as a compass to highlight your time here on earth.

Your loss has disoriented many of your friends and family. Even strangers are quite dismayed by the sudden ending of your young life. People from out of town that I barely know call me upon learning the news that you died. They offer condolences, and any help if needed.

Justin, the end of your earthly existence has sent shock waves throughout our town and beyond. Time has stood still, and we are reeling from the blow of your death. There are many broken-hearted people missing and loving you so, so much my dearest son.

Loving you beyond the depths that my heart has ever felt, dear Justin.

You were one of a kind.

Love,
Mom

INNER AND OUTER LAYERS

My dear Jai,

February 21, 2020

I'm going through the lovely floral arrangement from my birthday party. I notice as I remove the outer layers of wilted flowers, I get to the heart of the bouquet and find another layer of simplicity, and elegance that was hidden by the other blossoms and leaves.

Getting to the center through the many layers and finding more loveliness reminds me of life. When I go deep inside from the surface glories and experience the depths of silence, I have an even greater appreciation for the inner and outer brilliance of creation.

My love for you dear Justin is deep and profound and goes beyond anything this mother's heart has ever experienced. The love I feel for you pulsates throughout my heart in a concentrated form of strength and ease.

My love for you is complete.

Love,
Mom

THE SUBTLE VOICE OF SILENCE: MY SOUL

Dear Jai,

February 22, 2020

I enjoy the silence. Profound peace and tranquility emerge from the depths of its subtle voice: the voice of my soul that mere words cannot convey. There's no chance of tripping up the truth, no chance of misunderstanding what's being said when it comes from the wisdom of the soul: the delicate voice of pure intelligence.

There's so much to say to you, but more is felt in the quiet cloisters: a refuge from the chaos as I fall back into the all-knowing Self, again, and again, and again.

The language of the subtle voice of silence: my soul.

Loving you always,
Mom

IDENTIFYING YOU

Dear Jai,

February 22, 2020

My motherly love for you began when you were in my womb. You were still an abstract and yet very physical presence of yourself expanding inside of me. From the tiny seed of love your individuality sprouted and was birthed on the auspicious day of your new life on Earth.

Each stage of your incarnation found meaning and direction as you developed more of your genetic blueprint. Your wavy brown hair, big bright eyes, soft voice, tall presence, along with your discerning intellect, quick wit and fondness of nature expressed some of your persona. This is how I knew you.

Now you have moved beyond the human identity you once inhabited, but I still recognize you. The remnants of your imprint are still alive, although you're no longer in the form I'm familiar with. You are now an embodiment of light: brilliant, illuminating and radiant. The eternal essence of God's light is your new attire.

Every now and then my awareness glimpses through the refined perception of my senses: sight, sound, smell and touch. I appreciate your subtle and yet unforgettable presence.

This is a new way of identifying you, Jai. You will never be forgotten.

Love
Mother

INFINITY TO POINT

Dear Jai,

February 23, 2020

Riding the wave of love into the heart of God. My mind traverses the many layers of awareness till I arrive at the source of my Being, the silent abstract flow of stillness, the undercurrent that unifies all of creation. This is where we begin again and again, then our journey starts. Falling into the Self, moving consciousness onto It Self. From the infinite, eternal, boundless, never ending, inexhaustible and absolute field, we were created and found one another. From infinity to the point of our created incarnation our souls aligned. Out of the innumerable universes that exist, we were formed as humans and came to live upon planet Earth.

Jai, love brought you, Dad, Kel and me together. What a spectacular miracle. Having you in my life even for a short instant, I am forever grateful. The powerful force of our love brought us into each other's world and will again, someday, some way.

Love is the power,
Mom

BIG LIFE

Dear Jai,

February 26, 2020

Jai, you were never in the corner. Always in the spotlight of your family, friends and business partners. Women loved you and your girlfriend adored you and was very devoted to the relationship. Everyone enjoyed having you near. You were always positive and encouraging to be around.

My dear, dear son how could you with your big life, slip away in an instant, unnoticed? You left us behind and entered the next life: a new world, a new reality, a new awareness.

You had so many dreams, for yourself and others. A friend of yours recently reached out to your sister. This is what they said to her, "I'm thinking of your brother's passing. I loved him deeply; I'm crying as I'm writing this. We would talk for hours about our dreams and ambitions. We had big plans together. He told me I would be something special one day. He was one of the first people who made me believe it. I became V.P. of the company I work for. Its value went from $80,000 to a multimillion-dollar business. I was always thinking of him during this process. Just wanted to let you know how important his legacy is to me."

Jai, your life has meant so much to all of us.

I love you,
Mom

CREATING ORDER IN CHAOS

Dear Justin,

February 27, 2020

For me, writing is similar to cleaning house. It's my opportunity to put the messiness of life's traumatic events into some kind of neat and tidy order. Out of the entropy of the emotional chaos from the great shock of your death, comes the arrangement of my feelings. I attempt to put them into clear, concise, organized thoughts. Writing helps me make sense of the senseless and gives me an objective point of view. It cleans up the emotional dust that lingers in the corners of my mind and shines the light of clarity and coherence onto the disturbing reality of your passing.

Putting my emotions into words helps me step back and look through the lens of my grief, not only with my heart, but also with my intellect. Illuminating the distressed part of me and deeply examining the residual effects left behind from the shock waves of your passing, this is how I heal and continue to move forward in a life without you in it.

Loving you always,
Mom

THE EDGE

Dear Justin,

I am bound to you through the joy of honoring and loving you. This is my inspiration. I hear the echoing of the drums and feel the pulsating heartbeat of creation enlivening me to the depth of my being. My awareness reaches out to the edge of my boundaries; I am tickled to my core and the confines of hardened limitations are shaken loose. You have taken up residence in the subtle corners of my awareness. The karmic imprint of your life washes through my memory, and my love for you knows no bounds.

I love you,
Mom

OWNERSHIP

Dear Jai,

March 3, 2020

I am no longer who I used to be. My beliefs have loosened up, been rearranged and are more flexible, like a Japanese fan unfolding. There is a new paradigm of how to view life without you in it. I quietly watch and see how events naturally develop. Expectations of any kind seem to be a naive way to live and a sure way to experience further disappointments.

A personal truth that I must acknowledge, is that your death has impacted every aspect of my existence. On some level, what happened to you has also happened to me. There is no denying this. It has become a huge part of who I am. I have taken ownership of your passing. When you left, a big part of myself went with you and will stay that way till the day I die.

Loving you forever,
Mom

SHIVA'S EYES

Dear Jai,

March 4, 2020

Your time was up and your death was allowed to happen. In that instant your family's and friend's lives were altered and impacted forever by your passing.

In the Hindu scriptures, their Supreme Being, Lord Shiva, is represented in three different images. In one of the images, Shiva's eyes are half open, which symbolizes the cycle of life in process. In another image, his eyes are fully open, which signifies the beginning of creation. In the last image, his eyes are closed signaling the end or destruction of the universe.

On that fateful day of your death the Supreme Being must have had his eyes closed. I would say they were shut tight, how else could he have allowed your human incarnation to come to a sudden end?

When your breath ceased our worlds stood still, and we all gasped for life: for your life to return to you, and you to us.

The day that Shiva closed his eyes is the day you left us and we are absolutely heart broken. We are still gasping for air when we think of this sad day.

With a heavy heart,
Mother

A SWEET VISIT

Dear Justin,

March 5, 2020

I'm sitting with you in the fullness of nature outside of your godmother Ellen's house. We have driven over so she can see you. As we are waiting outside for her to come home, I'm aware of being surrounded by very tall trees and the scent of fresh brown earth. I'm sensing the abundance of nature all around me. I feel the greenery and look up and see a protective canopy of trees above us.

I'm aware that you have died, and in spite of that I am able to spend some time with you. Your presence feels real, but I know this is a dream. You're telling me you want to go to a party that you heard some pretty women will be there. I ask you, "How can you go to a party when everyone knows you died?" You don't respond.

It feels like a miracle to be with you if only for a moment in a very lively dream. I'm starting to feel tender and fragile since I know that you have died, and I will feel your loss when I wake up, but right now every fiber of my being is pulsating with so much love.

I go to the door of your godmother's home and find out she was there the whole time we were waiting for her. The dream is over and I wake up crying because you have disappeared. I want you back so badly. I won't let you go. You were my baby and as your mother I refuse to abandon my child.

I will stay with you in memory and continue sending my love to you each and every day, my dear son.

Love,
Mother

PHYSICALITY

Dear Justin,

March 6, 2020

The only thing missing between us is your physicality. Our love for one another is still lively; the feelings are deeply felt, but we both operate from very different perspectives of reality and we are worlds apart as well.

I am feeling like you are gone because you're no longer in a human being's body; this has changed our way of communicating. Speaking, seeing, touching and hearing you is more difficult. As humans our senses are part of the physical form and the conduit that is needed for us to interact with one another. I am deeply mourning the loss of this connection; I prefer you being a human since I am.

I can't say I know what you are experiencing on the other side of the veil. Being on the receiving end of you since you passed, and based on the feedback I have received from our family members and friends, it appears that there are some consistencies in when and how you want to connect with us. You come to us in what we call dreams, but when they are particularly vivid and clear, it's more of a visitation. You like to connect through music, nature, signs, telepathy, touch, humor, refined sight, light, special days and electricity. I remember it was morning and I was getting ready for the day. A big wave of grief came over me and I started to sob uncontrollably. The music on my YouTube playlist suddenly started to play, Todd Rundgren's, "I Saw the Light." That was not the next song on the list. I thought, "Well I can't argue with that."

You love feels huge, and has a transcendental quality to it. It's

194

big and pure and lifts us up. Your language is the language of the subtle. The communication happens quickly, and we must be alert to catch it. This is your new voice, your means of conversing with us.

Please continue to stay in touch.

Loving you forever,
Mom

FOR A MOMENT

Dear Justin,

March 8, 2020

Now you are free, somewhere in the celestial realms with a body of light. I'm still on Earth. I believe that in heaven we find ourselves infused with the joyfulness of God and we live a glorious existence.

I lost you, my dear son, when you gained heaven, so a big damper of gloom has been placed upon my feelings of joy. What a predicament we find ourselves in!

The event of your death has impacted us both very differently, hasn't it? On the days when the grief is particularly strong, I feel as though I am wearing a heavy coat of sorrow and my love is shaded in deep, somber hues of blue. I find myself in pensive thought, silently reflecting on those precious moments we once shared.

I remember when you were a new born baby. It was just for a brief moment with so much latent potential waiting to be revealed: a future where the unfoldment of the various expressions and the characteristics of your DNA would take form.

You were a young boy for a moment. Waking up to all the exciting activities that little boys like to engage in: catching frogs, mulberry picking, riding your bicycle and playing in the creek. There was still so much time for you to live your life and fulfill all your dreams.

You were a teenager for a moment with time to grow out of the tumultuous teen angst and develop into a grounded, confident man. It was also a time of building many life long friendships.

You were an adult for a moment: finding love and sharing your dreams with someone else, as well as refining your skills in business, and honing your creative and intellectual gifts to build a successful future.

All these precious moments were at the appropriate stages of your development in the course of your life. Each moment setting the platform for the next opportunity for you to grow and become your authentic self.

I love each and every moment of your sweet life.

Love,
Mom

IF YOU WERE STILL ALIVE

Dear Jai,

March 8, 2020

I dream about you, but you eventually disappear from my sight.

I say to you, "Why don't you linger a bit longer, I don't want you to fade away; I'm missing you."

My dear son, I'm always missing you.

A good friend of yours from California recently came to visit us. In my mind I was calling you up to tell you what a nice time we had with Riki and her boyfriend, Andrew. Your sister was also home for a visit. You may have been here with them as well, if you were still alive.

I saw some of your childhood friends at a local cafe the other night. I could see you having fun with them, catching up on life, eating some dinner and enjoying each other's company. It's what you would have been doing if you were home for a visit, if you were still alive.

Kel brought her puppy home with her when she was in town. We had such a sweet time with her new pup. You would have loved her. I could see you playing with her and the little one getting rambunctious with you as puppies generally do. It's what you would have been doing, if you were still alive.

I see your spirit participating in all of these activities as I super-impose the Justin that once lived as a part of them.

I visualize you in these settings as if you were still alive.

Love,
Mom

TOO FAST

Dear Justin,

March 10, 2020

As life moves on, I see how much being your mother
has meant to me.
The depth of that role has far surpassed anything I could
have expected it to be.
Now that you have passed, I promise to continue to love and
honor you, even if it comes in dark shades of blue.
I feel you more than ever, this bond between us that
I won't allow time or death ever sever.

What we once had, this life of joy since you were
my baby boy, is no longer to be, and yet at times I feel you
very close to me.
Even though you couldn't stay and it was your time
to go away,
I realize that nothing is meant to last, but it ended
much too fast.

Always loving you,
Mom

FINDING YOU

Dear Jai,

March 10, 2020

> As the pulsating music starts to silence,
> its primordial sounds are my guidance.
> From the world's discordant noise,
> I'm being led home to the source of my joys:
>   You.

Love,
Mom

I BELIEVE THE SOUL KNOWS

Dear Jai,

March 12, 2020

Many years ago, I had an astrological reading of our family's horoscopes done. By looking at our birth charts, the astrologer could determine the longevity of our lives, but for some reason I couldn't find your chart to bring with me to the meeting. The astrologer predicted that Dad, Kel and I would live well into our late 80's and 90's, but a prediction on the length of your life never took place.

Over the years a quiet little voice would nudge me, deep inside the back of my mind that you weren't going to live a long life, and that is why the reading didn't take place for you that day. I pushed that voice away time and again, only to realize that after your death my soul was trying to prepare me for your eventual demise.

I believe the soul knows.

The day before you passed away you called home to say "hi" to Dad and me. When I picked up the phone and heard your voice, my first thought was you sounded like you were on the "other side."

I said to myself, "What a crazy thought I'm having."

I pushed it away for the rest of the day and didn't give it my attention until the next day when you died.

It was not a crazy thought at all, but my soul was whispering into my awareness that you would soon be on the other side of life.

I believe the soul knows.

What is the soul and how does it know such things?

I believe the soul is a part of God that lives within each and every one of us. It's the spark of life that animates us and is the essence of who we are, our God Self. The soul is with us throughout our lifetime and continues with us into the afterlife; it is our immortal Self that never dies. I think our soul is a huge powerful energy, and that our human body can't contain the vibration of our whole soul, so just a portion of it incarnates with us in each lifetime. I feel the soul is the all-knowing part of our Self that assists us throughout life with knowledge and direction as we navigate through our human incarnation. We just need to be quiet and alert enough to hear its gentle whispers as it tries to prepare us for what we need to do next.

Perhaps this higher power is there so when difficult times in life arrive, I have the depth of knowingness it was decreed to be, and out of my control.

When we come into alignment with our soul, we come into alignment with the truth.

Loving you so much with my whole heart and soul.

Love,
Mother

NATURE BOY

Dear Jai,

March 13, 2020

Springtime is approaching. The buds on the trees are taking form and will be blooming in another month, and Mother Nature will be in full swing. She is shaking off the deep wintry slumber as she engages in painting her portraits of bright flowers with their intoxicating fragrances and colorful hues.

Yellow sunshine is warming our bodies and the frozen ground, is thawing. Magnificently shaded skies of blue serve as a backdrop to vibrant rainbows that appear after a heavy spring downpour. All the glories of the season will be upon us.

I see the world now through your eyes. I see your appreciation of how you loved to watch the blossoming of nature and everything around us coming back to life.

As a child, you loved jumping on the trampoline with the sprinkler nearby to cool you off, climbing trees, catching frogs, picking floral bouquets from our garden for me and playing cannonball with Dad in the neighborhood pool.

Mother Nature shimmers in her exalted state, illuminated and divine, heavenly and earthly.

God's nature is our nature.

You were my nature boy.

Loving you always,
Mom

REALITY SHIFT

Dear Jai,

All the people in your life had their own unique bond with you, and therefore, your passing has impacted each one of us quite differently.

I've been reflecting on Kelly and what she lost when you died. I realize that her grief has an additional layer of the sad reality of losing her only sibling and therefore, rendering her sibling-less.

In the thirty-four years of her life, you were a strong presence for thirty-one of them. A deep link of kinship formed during those formative years. You both had a fundamental influence on one another's development, and a lot of how you viewed the world was through each other's eyes.

This familial connection gave you two a sense of your roles in the family dynamic and a place in the order of life. Kel was your big sister and now she is an only child.

You shared your lives and valued friendships into your adult years: living together for some time in California and exploring its coastline. This was a big change from where you both were raised and a very special time in your growth towards independence.

When you died, your sister not only lost her baby brother, but also her other half that she journeyed from her childhood into adulthood with. Your earthly journey together has ended, and the sibling bond has been broken: as she knows it. The continuous thread of your daily lives, interwoven by the history you once shared, is no more. Now your relationship vibrates on a whole new level of existence that calls for a finer degree of awareness and appreciation.

This is a huge reality shift for Kelly.

Love,
Mother

MY TEARS

Dear Jai,

March 24, 2020

I have been thinking about what crying is and what it does for me. I have been doing much of it since you died. I must admit that when I'm sobbing, a part of me feels good; a lot of pent of tension is released. This is my way to self heal: my feel-good medication therapy, minus the drugs.

Chemicals are released when we cry from sadness: endorphins and oxytocin. The body produces these comforting chemicals in response to our unhappiness. God that is so beautiful; She thought of everything! How kind to soothe us as we weep. My tears are a reflection of the grief emotion from my broken heart, and this heart needs a good release.

Since you died, I find my tears are more profuse. At times it's as though a waterfall has exploded, and my tears pour forth liberally; they even feel wetter, if that is possible. I allow the floodgates to open and my tears come cascading down onto my face. This is my way of expressing that I am deeply missing you.

May each and every one of my tears drop into God's universal ocean of a Mother's love for her departed child. May they bring comfort and joy to you and please, always know I hold you in the highest esteem and you are worth every one of my tears.

Love you,
Mother

A NEW START

Dear Jai,

March 25, 2020

First a sigh and then I cry. It's going on nine
months long; perhaps it's time to sing another song.
I want you to stay with me, please soothe my
broken heart, I just don't like us being so far apart.
Photos of us so happy and carefree, who would of thought
this would ever be?
If I left here and went far away, could I find you on
another day?
In another place separate from this time,
and we could be together again, me as your sister,
mother or friend.
In a new reality with no more tears, a chance for
me to release all my fears.
A kinder world I would enter, of only love and joy,
a place where I would find my baby boy.

Love is the nectar pouring from my heart,
my libation to the Creator to give us a brand
new start.

Love always,
Mom

SNIPPETS OF TIME

Dear Jai,

March 30, 2020

I am lying awake in bed. The fatigue of slumber is not descending upon me in a timely manner. With my eyes wide open I find myself looking into another place in time.

You are walking down the street in Santa Cruz. Dad and I are out for a visit with you. You're wearing sweat pants and a gray knit top, another one of your favorite colors. I'm watching you walk; you're happy and carefree. Chatting along as we are heading over to your much loved Asian restaurant.

You are my little boy, now grown into a young man. I'm noticing your gait, even and fluid. You're wearing your black sneakers. What a handsome stature you have grown into! You possess a kind, loving and sweet energy. This figure of a man I'm watching once grew inside of me. I was part of your formation. It's hard to believe how fast time has flown by, or perhaps it's how fast we move through time.

I can see that your happiness is a continuation of the same happiness you had as a child. You carried it with you your whole life. You felt secure and loved. I'm smiling as I am watching this scene on the movie screen of my life. First time that I can reminisce and feel good.

Perhaps some progress is being made, well at least in this moment.

Loving you so much,
Mother

NOW THAT YOU ARE FREE

Dear Jai,

April 6, 2020

How are things going to go, now that you are gone?
Where are they going to be, now that you are free?
When love and grief are joined at the hip, I realize
it's an emotional trip.

My new companion with loving you, is the deep void
of missing too.

This receiver needs a clear reception of what is to be,
at this point it evades me.

In the stillness I watch as life unfolds; perhaps I will
eventually make some inroads.

This vessel is completely filled with thoughts of you,
love for you, and grieving too.

It all revolves around you.

Love you always,
Mom

EDGY LIVING

Dear Jai,

April 7, 2020

My world has been shaken up again and again. I need you to give me some hope; an angel or two would do. Please assist me on this crazy journey in an atmosphere that warrants guidance in proceeding towards an uncertain future.

Lines are crossed.

Anything can go now, since you are gone, you proved that.

It's edgy living now. I'm at the ledge that points to the beyond of no more boundaries.

Where do we go from here?

I watch quietly through my tears as the mystery continues to unfold.

Loving you,
Mother

INTO THE SELF

Dear Jai,

I stop and stare into a memory of you as you move through my awareness. Life comes and goes as I listen for your gentle voice. There is a delicate wall between us. We are on opposite sides of this subtle wall, but the golden thread of our love keeps us connected; this is my lifeline to you.

As the great facade melts away, I close my eyes, falling in from the outside, effortlessly going inward. Pulling back to the Self to find you here with me, my loving son, you remain with me through it all. I come back to the place where you are.

Your radiance resides deep within the golden chambers of my heart and I am home.

Loving you always,
Mother

HIGHER LOVE

Dear Jai,

April 13, 2020

As I'm facing your death, the physical death of Justin Malloy, my love for you has reached new heights. You have given me a higher love.

My love transcends the boundaries of my world and has followed you into the heavens, where you now reside. Loving you into the heavenly realms has given my love a different quality. Your new status as a light being has given my love a divine status.

My love for you is relentless. It knows no limits; it never rests. This love is lively and super fluid and traverses beyond my atmosphere. It has a will of its own.

My love for you, my dear son, is complete and full. It overflows like a magnificent ocean bursting forth from my heart.

You have given me a higher love, and I thank you.

Loving you always,
Mother

A DELICATE TIME OF TRANSITION

Dear Jai,

April 15, 2020

The glowing quality of your face was the first thing I noticed about you when you came home for Mother's Day, May 10, 2019. In your eyes, I saw a soft radiance emanating from your soul reflecting off your face: smooth and luminous, a picture of perfect health. In your smile, you gave forth the love that was exuding from your Being: kind and tender, generous and full. The whites of your eyes were glimmering with light, your hair soft and fine, and your complexion: flawless.

Everything about your appearance was strikingly soft and healthy. To be honest, I was surprised to see you looking so well. For years you had been working yourself to the bone and could have been more rested. In our previous visits I had noticed you were getting a few premature lines under your eyes and you looked a bit tired, but still good. This time, no sign of aging or fatigue appeared in your face. I told you how good I thought you looked, and you thanked me.

Little did I know that your soul was preparing for your transition into the celestial field, and it was starting to show itself to my inner eye. Gazing into your field of brilliance, I was seeing the shimmering light of the heavenly world where you would soon transition to. I was witnessing you changing from a human being into a full-time celestial being.

Your outward appearance looked the same to all who saw you, but I saw the light casting your future identity, as your soul was preparing for your heavenly journey.

Your outer shell would soon be removed.

This was a passage in space and time where you were living, so close to the edge of life and death. It was a precious and delicate moment, and one I will never, ever forget.

This was the last time I saw you before you passed away six weeks later.

Loving your beautiful brilliance,
Mother

ON AND ON

Dear Jai,

April 15, 2020

I find myself absorbed in missing you. My love is constantly searching for you. The power of this love leads me on. I go deep within and there I discover your essence; my instincts know where to go. I feel for you and see the doorway to your soul is love. Shedding my pride, I arrive without a sound. You have transcended the senses, but for me it is what I have as my compass to find you in: music, nature, in my joy and sadness, in my breath, in the light and in my darkest hours.

My life is sustained in loving you, as each moment slips into the next, and on and on.

Deeply loving you,
Mom

SPARKLES OF HEAVEN

Dear Jai,

April 17, 2020

I am thinking about your final moments on Earth. I put my arms around you and hug you so deep and long. I hold you and don't want to let go. I realize it was your time to go home and I will always be with you, no matter what. Even though you are no longer in human form, our souls are united. Our love for one another transcends the physical facade.

I still need you; I still miss you, but apparently you had a new journey to go on, you with the angels by your side.

On a sunny California day you slipped away. Moving from time through the portal to timelessness; this is where you now reside. As I'm writing this to you the clouds in the gray, rainy sky momentarily disappear. The sun comes out and illuminates the rain drenched leaves, and they glisten with a beautiful sparkle of heaven, and I know it's you saying "hello."

"Hello backatcha."

Love always,
Mother

HEART HUG

Dear Jai,

April 25, 2020

I sit in quiet mourning, and a memory of you comes to my awareness. The memory of when you were a nine-month-old baby surfaces. We are sitting on the sand at the beach in South Carolina. Your sun-bleached hair curls and your round little cherub face crinkles up and smiles at me. Your laughter echoes through me.

Your face is broken out in a rash. I assume it is something in my breast milk you are reacting to. Probably the seafood I'm eating. Although you are red and rashy, it doesn't bother you. Playing in the sand with your pail and shovel, you're content.

I'm reveling in the moment and wish it would continue, but it gently fades away. I love these moments.

I feel the physical structure of my heart expand around you and it gives my little baby a hug.

My love for you will always be in a perpetual state of hugging you, my sweet baby boy.

Love,
Mom

YOUR MEMORIAL SITE

Dear Jai,

April 25, 2020

Your memorial site is on the loop trail by our home. It is pretty much completed. It's a welcoming resting spot for the people walking along the path. I have received positive feedback from friends and acquaintances. Folks seem happy seeing what was created for you.

Next a tree will be planted along with some prairie grasses. The tree I picked out is called, Sugar Thyme. The berries stay on them all year long. That makes me happy that the deer will have berries to eat during the cold winter months. I call it, "Jai's Giving Tree."

I feel the tribute memorializing you is good reflection of who you were; always giving, solid and strong like the boulder we attached the beautiful plaque onto. A place to share with others that need to rest and have a seat on the ornate Dragon Fly benches from your godmother Ellen and her family.

Most of all it's out in the middle of nature where you loved to spend your time.

Loving you,
Mother

MUCH LOVE ON A SUNDAY AFTERNOON

Dear Jai,

April 26, 2020

Today I was remembering your passing. It was Sunday afternoon; the sun was shining on you, and God was calling you from the heavens to come back home. That day you left your body behind, and with your guardian angel by your side, you embarked on a new journey. Your human incarnation was over.

We were at Natural Grocer when Dad received the call from Kelly that you had drowned. I was looking at him, not yet knowing what she was saying, but I saw his body tense up and nearly collapse, and his voice became agitated. Once he told me, we immediately exited the store with a shopping cart full of food left behind.

Dad was on the phone sitting outside on a bench calling the hospital to get information. I went into our car and was screaming and crying with all-consuming grief. A woman came over to see what was wrong. I told her you died, and she said she wished she had some Valium to give me. I was stunned. A moment of sheer insanity would be an understatement.

We finally returned home in a state of utter despair. It was the longest car ride of my life.

By evening most everyone knew you had passed away.

As your body was laid to rest in California, loved ones gathered around our home in Iowa to help us with the trauma of your sudden departure. With their loving, compassionate hearts, our family and friends had come to cushion the blow as we found ourselves in the midst of heavy grief.

Your sweet cousin, Meara, sat next to me. She was listening to the stories I was telling about your life and she wrote a poem to you.* She read it to the group. We were all amazed by her clarity and insight into your transition.

A nourishing cocoon of healing love was building around us.

Love always knows to show up when desperately needed. Love knows exactly where to go and when to arrive. Love cannot be suppressed.

I bow down to Love and surrender my life to upholding the dignity of this powerful force of nature.

Thank you, dear Love.

Love you,
Mom

*Meara's poem, "For My Cousin Justin," is in the beginning of the book.

ALMOST A YEAR

Dear Jai,

April 26, 2020

I remember when you were new,
actually born the day you were due.
It was an excellent time,
our life was sweet and all was fine.

I always thought you would stay,
but instead you went away.

When the music plays, I think of the days navigating
the misty haze of life,
love was our guidance through any strife.

And now you have walked through another door
and seem to be no more.

Out there somewhere very close, but just not here,
You're gone now for almost a year.

Love,
Mom

LIVELY SACRED SPACES

Dear Jai,

April 29, 2020

I was recently up in your bedroom meditating. The room is quite lively with your presence of who you were and who you are now.

I'm sitting in your chair and reflecting on the different chapters of your life from infancy into your adult years. I'm admiring the many photos of you on display. Every photo captures the highlights of your time here on Earth and they radiate so much joy. Snapshots of you sitting on Santa's lap at Dad's company Christmas party, making silly faces for the camera with your sister, and celebrating Dad's mayoral victory with your family.

I go through your closet and take a deep inhale of your clothes. I am happy I can still smell your wonderful scent on them, so much of you left behind.

This is the space you grew and developed into your teens and visited for one last time six weeks before you passed away.

I come to this space to feel your human side and quietly reminisce about our life together. The distinctive impression of Justin, the you I once knew is quite palpable and I still need to feel that.

At the same time, I feel your subtle essence all around the room. Your soul is very much alive and here with me. I knew you as a human and now I'm learning to know you in your celestial form as well. My body tingles with warm memories and a gentle peace embraces me.

Your room has become a sacred place to pay tribute to you and where the remnants of your humanity are still lingering, with your spirit right alongside of it telling the story of my son.

Always loving you,
Mom

SO MANY MEMORIES,
SO MANY FEELINGS

Dear Jai,

May 3, 2020

You and Kel were each other's best friend. Always looking out for the other, and being a strong support system was a lively part of your sibling dynamic. You were one another's biggest fan. You included each other in your social lives and didn't let the 3 ½-year age difference create a distance. Your friends were Kel's and vice versa. She loved having her younger brother around. There was a mutual respect between the two of you. It was a harmonious sibling friendship and a joy to see it blossom and grow into your adult years. My sister Denise and I had a similar relationship.

There was never any distinction between my love for the two of you, it always was and still is, one love.

Justin, since you passed away there are times I feel your radiance showering upon me. I bask in the light of who you are now. Your essence is the same, only now you're no longer in your human shell. I feel you in the core of my Being and relish each moment of your presence.

My dear friend sent me an E-Card to acknowledge that today is Bereaved Mother's Day. She lost her only child seven years ago. In the card the music of Ave Maria is playing as a lovely floral arrangement of flowers grow fuller and fuller as the melody continues on. This song struck a deep chord within me. It was the same song another dear friend of mine sang at your funeral service. I have never heard of Bereaved Mother's Day and didn't know such a day existed, as my tears swell up, and start dripping onto this page.

So many feelings to feel and emotions to navigate through in this new reality of life without you.

Loving you always,
Your bereaved Mother

SPRINGTIME PANDEMIC

Dear Jai,

May 6, 2020

As I am taking my morning walk, I couldn't help but notice the delicate aromatic scent in the air. The flowering trees, bushes and floral groupings are in full bloom, and their pervasive fragrances are most delightful. The birds are singing their good morning songs. The wide open, blue Iowa sky with its huge white, billowy clouds float above me. The once brown, wintry grass has turned a vibrant shade of green.

Simultaneously the world is going through a health crisis. The expression "pandemic" has become a commonplace household word. The outbreak of a potentially deadly virus threatens us. News reports are rife with fear and stories of loss of lives is plenty. A dark cloud of disease assaults humanity: a big contrast to the dynamic spirit and vivacity of the Springtime season. Despite the pandemic, Mother Nature has come along dressed in her joyful and flamboyant attire lifting me up in her Springtime finest. Thank you, dear Mother.

Our state leaders are encouraging us to stay home and self-iso-late in order to stop the viral ravage. Big cities are setting curfews, folks are losing their jobs, schools are closing, and students are learning remotely via teleconference. Thousands are dying from the virus, especially the elderly. Factories are breeding grounds for transmitting the disease due to the close proximity of their work conditions, and they are shutting down. Families are sitting in their cars for hours waiting on food lines in order to feed themselves.

A new way of living has emerged. There's a huge phase transition taking place. It's forcing us to press the reset button and learn how to live life in a different way. We are being given the opportunity to be more inward and self-reflective. Nature is telling us to slow down, stay home with our family, cook delicious meals, get creative, meditate and simplify our lives.

It is also a time to realize how fragile life is and the junction point between life and death is very lively right now for everyone. Our mortality is staring us in our faces and making us uncomfortable.

Through it all the natural rhythm of nature's cycle continues to move forward. She is birthing a new season, and nothing can get in the way of the life she is springing forward.

Jai, I know how much you loved nature and I think my heightened awareness and deepened appreciation of this Springtime season is due to you. You will continue to live within me.

The best part of you resides in my heart and soul, and I thank you, my son.

Loving you so much,
Mother

MORE QUESTIONS

Dear Jai,

May 7, 2020

Life continues on without you.

This is my first spring with you living in heaven, but the seasons come and go even though you are gone from Earth. It seems strange to me that the world can continue without you in it and my broken heart hasn't crushed humanity with the weight of its grief. For me, each and every day is all about you. I've learned first-hand, the hard way, that the infinite stream of life continues onward no matter what. It is a powerful force. It is bigger than your death and my grief and yet lovingly embraces all of it and so much more.

Jai, where did the love in your heart go when you passed away and your life on Earth ceased to be? Did your love expand as wide and huge as your cosmic Beingness now that you no longer live within the confines of your body? Did your love merge with all the love in God's great sea of universal love? Do you still feel personal love for your family and friends? Do you still have a personal identity of Justin Malloy that is lingering around and yet simultaneously is existing within your universal status? Are you one big unbounded Being of brilliant light ? Have you merged with many other souls that you share a deep connection to and have been together for all eternity?

Is there a part of my soul that hasn't incarnated and still resides in heaven with you? Am I with you right now in heaven and just don't know it because my awareness is blocked from this multi-dimensional reality? Is all this grief silly, and I need to get a grip on it?

My dear son, now you are the one with the answers of things spiritual and divine, so I look to you for guidance as a way to mend my grieving heart.

Loving you so much,
Mother

THE ROAD I TRAVEL

Dear Jai,

The wind blows against my face; hard and cold,
my teardrops are delicate and warm as they
gently caress my cheek.
They are opening me up to what I can't deny,
as I walk along my chosen path.
This heart of mine is ancient and eternal,
it holds the memories of all that has
come before, what is now and what is
yet to be: simultaneously happening
in a flash.
This is where I find myself.
This is the road I now travel as I surrender to
what is.
This is my highway to the light, to God's
light, to your light.

Loving the light.

Love,
Mother

A YEAR AGO TODAY

Dear Jai,

Mother's Day, May 12, 2020

A year ago today, you came home to celebrate Mother's Day. What a beautiful gift you gave me. Thank-you!

A year ago today, we spoke, hugged, and laughed together.

A year ago today, you were home in the secure arms and warm embrace of your family with Dad, Kel and me, feeling the love we feel for one another and enjoying precious moments of silence.

A year ago today, we sat together, ate our meals, chatted about life, watched T.V., and enjoyed each other's company.

A year ago today, Kelly and you reminisced about your years growing up together as you drove to all the spots you frequented in your youth. Driving over to Crow Creek where you and your friends hung out, going over to your school and remembering your teachers and the sporting events you played in and the old putt-putt golf course. You shared a life together.

A year ago today, you saw your uncle/godfather Ken and your cousins. You had a sweet relationship with them. We ate a pre-Mother's Day dinner at their lovely home. You would say good-bye to them that night for the last time.

A year ago today, you slept in your bed, woke up the next morning, walked down the stairs, hugged me one final time and flew back to California.

A year ago today, was you last visit home.

What a holy and sacred time it was for all of us. A time of great change was upon you. Living on the edge of life and death is a powerful junction point. A point in time like none other.

Six weeks later you passed away.

Loving you so deeply,
Mother

PLEASE WAIT

Dear Jai,

May 17,2020

As your soul was preparing to exit your body, it was starting to show itself, the big Self, the Self that is your God-Self.

The many layers of illusion of the great facade that blinds us from the truth of a greater reality was being revealed. Seeing into the depth of your Being has impacted me. It has brought me the consolation that I need as a mother that has lost her son. It has confirmed my belief that we are Beings of light housed in a human body, having an Earthly experience until it's time to shed our skin and return to our heavenly home. It happened to you and will eventually happen to me.

Will you please wait for my arrival, and we can start a brand new day together?

Loving you my dear, dear son,
Mother

THANK-YOU FOR YOUR SERVICE

Dear Jai,

May 20, 2020

Thank-you for your service. Thank-you for the role you played in being an authentic human being. Thank-you for coming to planet Earth and being such a wonderful son and serving your time here for thirty-one years. Thank-you for serving your family with so much love and appreciation. Thank-you for being a loving and respectful son to Dad. Thank-you for being a devoted and supportive brother to Kelly. Thank-you for coming home for Mother's Day and honoring me in that way; that served my heart quite well. Thank-you for being such a good friend to all your buddies and always being there for them. Thank-you for your kindness to animals and your constant care and concern for many years to your epileptic cat, Tucker. Thank-you for serving your business, your partners and clients with so much honesty, integrity and passion. Thank-you for trailblazing an industry that needed truth and legitimacy to enter into the 21st century. Thank-you for raising the standards of a product that can be of service in helping people that are ill. Thank-you for dedicating yourself to what you believed is the truth and wouldn't compromise your standards. Yours was a personal and local service you gave to those around you: your family, friends, community and state.

Thank-you, my dear son, for being your own man.

Love,
Mom

MY CHILDREN

Dear Jai,

May 21, 2020

I am swimming in the ocean of love. I feel so deeply into you and your sister. Your photos sit upon my dresser next to my bed. I have the most sacred part of my heart near me as I sleep at night: my children.

I have a large painting depicting Divine Mother standing behind the photos. She is looking over Her children. She gave me the gift of you and Kelly and I thank Her.

My heart expands beyond this physical organ with so much love that every fiber of my being pulses with deep emotion and many memories of our life together, holding Kelly in my arms right after her birth, feels surreal. I'm finally a mother after my still-born loss of Baby Boy Malloy. Then you come along 3 1/2 years later completing our family unit.

I reach into my soul and find us as one united entity. No more duality; that's the grand illusion.

I'm riding this wave for as long as I can while my grief over your death momentarily subsides, and I can see beyond all the limitations my mind tricks me into believing as the truth.

I love you,
Mother

WHAT IS IT LIKE?

Dear Jai,

June 2, 2020

What will it be like when I go to heaven? Will you be there to assist me on my journey as my soul is exiting the body? Leaving it far behind and allowing it to merge back into Mother Earth, as we fly away to the heavens together.

Justin, will I recognize you? You won't be in the body I have grown accustomed to seeing you in. Will our all-pervasive love that transcends form, space, and time, be the eternal link of familiarity and the recognition that you are my Jai? You lived with me in the 21st century as my son and me as your mother.

What will we do once we are reunited? Will we be visiting the various heavenly realms and you will introduce me to all the amazing beings of light that you met while I was still on Earth as a human? Will we go to different universes and help others with whatever gifts we have to share?

My dear, son, since you went away a huge part of myself is no longer here. My mind is steeped in thoughts and questions about where you are, what you are doing, and what heaven is like. I hear it feels like home, and yet we live our lives fearing death because we have forgotten our experience of heaven. Living in the density of Earth has infringed upon our conscious mind from remembering this glorious place.

It's quite an interesting play of forgetting and then remembering, isn't it?

Love,
Mother

FULL CIRCLE

Dear Justin,

June 13, 2020

I remember giving birth to you. You completed our family; from three to four, I didn't want for anymore. I remember your childlike innocence, loving hugs, your garden picked bouquets on those sweet, hot summer days. I remember your bright, handsome face, radiating love and grace; soft and tender, all I could do was joyfully surrender to being your mother and your friend till the very end. I remember distant thoughts that perhaps your time here may be short, but really, I never thought...

At the end of my Earthly existence, God will send Her angels to come take me home, and ask what was the high point of my life,

I'll have to say, "Heeding the call to be your mother. To love you so deeply and completely. I gave to you and you gave to me. Our love came full circle in the endless continuum of life, and that has become the thrill of it all." How sweet is that!

My love to you,
Mom

SINCE YOU LEFT

Dear Justin,

June 14, 2020

Chords are struck quite deeply, their resonance pulsates throughout my being with reverberating thoughts of you as I reflect on our time together. You passed through heaven's door, leaving this Earth, your family and friends far behind. A very sudden exit it was.

I realize though, that since you left, I must continue to live, even though you died. I must continue to give when so much is gone. I must continue to find fulfillment when a big part of me is empty. And since you left, I must continue to love, despite my broken heart.

Loving you so very much,
Mother

A SONG FROM THE PAST
IS PLAYING IN MY HEAD

Dear Jai,

August 10, 2020

I woke up this morning with a song from the past playing in my head. It's called, "Darkness, Darkness" and, Jesse Colin Young from the Youngbloods wrote and sang it. It came out when I was 16 in 1969.

I searched and found the song on YouTube and played it. The song had a video accompanying it of the Vietnam War. I found the lyrics in the song mesmerizing:

> Darkness darkness, be my pillow
> Take my head and let me sleep
> In the coolness of your shadow
> In the silence of your dream
>
> Darkness darkness, hide my yearning
> For the things that cannot be
> Keep my mind from constant turning
> Towards the things I cannot see now
> Things I cannot see now
> Things I cannot see

It continues on.

After listening to the song and watching the video of young, tired soldiers with their heads hung down grieving their buddies that were killed in action, I became quite emotional. I suddenly felt the sadness of the mothers that lost their sons during this war. Their loss was also my loss. I realize that we are all united in the hearts of our motherhood. My motherhood was also grieving for the young weary soldiers so far from home and missing the warm embrace of love from their family. Young men whose parents taught them to be kind and good people, are now trained to kill other young men.

I think about you. If you had been alive during the Vietnam War, and if you had to go off and fight, this would have been your song. My young son would be looking for a reprieve from the insanity of killing and need a warm blanket of darkness to let him sleep. The darkness would provide a cushion in the quiet corners to go inside. A chance to escape the inescapable reality of the horrors of war.

I reflected on the time during the war when I attended an evening candlelight vigil at Salisbury Park with several of my friends. We walked silently in a line with thousands of other young people to pay our respects to the young men that died. It was also a plea to end the war that went from 1955-1975.

Everything goes much deeper into my heart now. I feel everything because I am always feeling you and the profundity of this love sensitizes me to all of life.

Love,
Mother

FINAL ACT

My dear love,

Jai's birthday, August 11, 2020

At first you crawl the stairs,
giggling with laughter without any cares.
Your little baby body so young and fragile,
and yet surprisingly strong and agile.
Having so much fun going up and down,
if I would say, no, you would give me a frown.

Next you would climb the trees,
sweet summer days with a gentle breeze,
sitting with Mother Nature and the bees,
ever so silently.
Tree heights scaled without any fright;
this was my little boy's delight.

A golden brilliance emanating all around you,
from Justin to Jai,
you would become one day.

This was your life, no dress rehearsal,
playing your final act, then becoming universal.

Loving you so very much,
Mother

THANKSGIVING

Dear Jai,

November 29, 2020

This year your absence from Thanksgiving was painfully felt. My sadness was strong, and I shed many tears on the day.

With the Covid-19 pandemic raging throughout our country, Dad and I didn't go to celebrate the holiday with your sister as we had hoped. We spent the day by ourselves at home. Your father and I felt a deep void of emptiness without our children, and nothing could fill it, no matter how much turkey we ate!

The day after Thanksgiving Dad tested positive for Covid-19. He feels fine and appears to have an asymptomatic case of the virus. I tested negative. Even so, life has definitely become more tense. I feel like we are on the edge to somewhere unknown since you went away. Each day is a bit precarious and going out to the grocery store is a potential health risk.

A huge phase transition threatens the world since Covid-19 struck humanity. For me the transition hit when I watched my beloved mother take her last breaths in 2018, and a few months later I was diagnosed with a recurrence of breast cancer. Then in 2019, four months after my surgery, you died. Seven months later the pandemic broke out.

I realize I have been experiencing my own personal pandemic and huge losses for quite some time. In some way they have prepared me for the Covid-19 pandemic. Many people around the world are experiencing sudden losses of loved ones to the virus. We all share this global challenge together.

I understand all of these intense events as a powerful force in my growth as a human being. They have given me the opportunity to go deep inside myself and harness the stillness underlying the constant changes that take place in the relative field of creation. As awful as it looks from the outside, blessings are found in these challenges. I truly believe this, no matter how grief stricken my days may get.

What a wild ride life has become. It has been daunting, but certainly not boring.

Love,
Mom

GOOD MEDICINE

Dear Jai,

I find myself going out in the cold weather and taking brisk mile long walks.

Taking deep inhales and exhales as I go along the tree lined street is invigorating. I no longer find my body tensing up and cringing in the cold temperatures, but instead feel exhilarated.

When I'm in this outdoor, brisk walking state of mind, I feel you. The fresh air opens me up, and clears out my senses. Once I am in that space of clarity, I can appreciate your subtle essence that has merged with nature.

Walking and breathing in the fresh, crisp air is moving in step with your presence, and that I find to be good medicine.

Love,
Mom

YOUR ANCESTORS

Dear Jai,

December 4, 2020

I'm reflecting on your great grandparents, Vincent Bica and Providenza Romano. They were good-hearted, hard working people steeped in family traditions and values and this laid a strong foundation for their future generations. I am grateful to them for that. I loved them both very much and it was a sad day when they were no longer with us.

They immigrated from Italy to America when they were children, arriving on a large ship coming into the New York Harbor of Ellis Island. This is where they would find love and success and would live out the rest of their lives in various counties around the New York area.

You had similar features and characteristics of your great grandfather, Vincent: the bridge of his nose and hairline. Like you, he was a successful businessman, owning his own auto repair shop and gas station. Having grown up poor in a foreign country, this was a huge accomplishment for him. He liked to share his good fortune with his family. When I was a young girl, every summer he would take twenty-two of us on oceanside vacations and each Christmas his gift to all was another share in the stock market. Like him, you were generous, smart, motivated, and liked being your own boss.

He met your great grandmother, Providenza through her brother who was his good friend. They fell in love, married, had four children and lived a comfortable life.

I grew up calling her Nana.

Nana was born in Palermo, Italy in the late 1800's. When I

was a young woman, she told me a sweet story of why her mother, Anna, named her Providenza.

The story goes that before Nana was born, the town of Palermo was having a difficult time with the seasonal harvest, along with a general lack of prosperity for the townspeople. Everyone was struggling. Her mother told her that right after she gave birth to her, everything started to turn around and the town began to flourish, hence the inspiration for naming her daughter Providenza. Her mother took this as a sign that her daughter's birth encouraged God's providence for the people of Palermo, providing blessings of protection and comfort for the townsfolk.

Visiting my grandparents was always a treat for me, my siblings and cousins. They owned a huge house in the upper part of New York. This is where all their families would gather for holidays and special occasions. I remember Nana in the kitchen standing over a pot of gravy, cooking up a batch of pasta and many other delicious Italian dishes while singing opera.

After I moved to Iowa, I made sure to call her every few weeks. I remember after one of our conversations, I had the realization it would be our last. I decided that you and I should take a trip out East to pay her a visit. You were only three years old at the time. I made reservations to fly out the following week. Unfortunately, during that time she suddenly came down with pneumonia. She died the following week. We arrived in time for her funeral. Nana was eighty-eight years old.

I wish your great grandparents had lived to meet you in your adult years. I am certain your great grandfather Vincent and you would have had some lively conversations and debates about business, politics and religion. I think you would have learned a lot from him and I know for sure you would have loved great grandmother Providenza's authentic Italian cooking.

It must have been a special reunion with them when you met again in heaven.

Love,
Mom

MORNING EXCITEMENT

Dear Jai,

December 5, 2020

Upon awakening in the sweetness of the morning, a feeling of excitement is resting in my solar plexus. This has been going on for many years, but disappeared when you died, and now its resurfacing.

A childlike feeling of wonder energizes me throughout my day. It persists even in the darkness of my grief and the crazy world events that are taking place.

An old friend has come back to say, "Hey remember me? I never really left, but you have been needing time to grieve your son's death. The grief got so big, it squeezed me out, but I think you are now ready to allow mourning your son and enthusiasm for life to coexist." Like the lotus flower that is rooted in muddy water, finds its way pushing upward through the murky environment greeting the day as a magnificent flower. The light of a new dawn is blossoming.

Even though I am totally heartbroken over your death, it does get somewhat easier. The grip of grief slowly, gently, loosens its hold for longer spans of time.

It's good to feel the wonder of each day and this emotion of childlike excitement once again.

Love always,
Mom

WATCHING MY GRIEF

Dear Jai,

December 13, 2020

I'm sitting quietly when I suddenly find myself watching the emergence of my grief. This time it didn't have an emotion of sadness or a particular memory of you attached to it like it usually does. The action seemed more methodical in its delivery, as I was watching the unfoldment of my grieving process.

Out of nowhere, I find that grief comes to the forefront of my awareness and moves forward gripping my attention and then my tears automatically begin to flow. I watch this lively energy working its way through me in the quiet sanctuary of my inner stillness, and I'm somewhat amused in its pursuit. I surrender and allow it to go on for as long as it must.

My tears are a gentle cleansing, washing through me, and I honor them. Eventually my grief subsides, the tears dry up, and the moment passes.

Today the dynamic play of the unfoldment of my grieving process revealed itself to me.

Thank you

Love,
Mom

PERSONAL JOURNEY

Dear Jai,

December 13, 2020

I would like to address the people who pity my loss. I ask you to, "Please let it go." I never want my loss to cause you the distress or pain that accompanies the emotion of pity. Your loving compassion will suffice.

Also, no need to worry about me if I suddenly get chocked up when Jai's name comes up in conversation. It's okay for us to speak about him, and if I start to swell up with emotion, that's fine.

I want to feel every nuance of the grieving process and allow it to move through me in the most natural and organic way that is appropriate. This is not a time to stifle my feelings, but to let them flow so they can continue to loosen up and move out the weight of my sadness. I am not soliciting ways to forget my son's death or suppress the emotions that go along with this experience.

Nor do I want to wallow in the bottomless pit that one can fall into when losing a child. Being told, "The worst thing that can happen to a parent is their child dying," is not what I need to hear. I already know that and don't need any further confirmation of this reality.

Everything I am doing thus far on this journey of Jai's passing, is my own authentic way to grieve him, grow from it, and move forward.

This is my intensely, personal journey of mourning and figuring it out as I go along.

Thank you.

Love,
Mom

ALTAR OF MY LOVE

Dear Jai,

December 20, 2020

On the altar of my love, I place before you my blossoming heart. It grows and expands with each passing day. I take a pause and bow down to God and you, my dear son, with my floral offering as an expression of my hopes and dreams. I present this pink rose, my piece of heaven, and all that is contained within. I believe in it. Its beauty is graceful, honest and true. I'm delighted to stand with you on the altar of the Divine.

I love you,
Mom

BJ OR AJ

Dear Jai,

December 20, 2020

Since your death I arrange life and its numerous events into a timeline of before or after you died.

If it was before Jai died, (BJ), then I revel in the fine moments of your earthly presence with the knowledge that you were still a human being, living and breathing on planet Earth, along with my many memories. You were still a part of the day-to-day events of living life with me in this world as my son, and I find great comfort in that.

If it was after you passed away, then it's after Jai, or (AJ), and the moment is tinged with sadness. This sadness arises because I can no longer share with you the events, episodes, and social or political phenomena that constantly occurs on a daily basis in my world. The incident of your death has impacted the sharing we once had as mother and son. A shade of gray has left its filmy residue on the lens I view life through, since you are no longer an active, dynamic part of it.

Bottom line, I still really miss you.

I look at photos of you on Instagram and check the dates when they were taken and I count how much more time you had left.

Sunday, June 30, 2019 is the starting point of my life after Jai.

As I view your photos I look into your eyes, face, smile, and demeanor to see what you looked like five years, one year, six months, or a few days before you died. I think to myself, "This is how Justin appeared a few days before he would leave his body behind and go back to heaven. This is his expression, this is the plaid shirt that he wore, this is Justin eating dinner out with his friends," and so on. I want to see how you appeared back then with the present knowledge I now possess in the aftermath of your death. I look for any telltale signs or omens somewhere in your visual aspect. I didn't find any clues.

Before and after your death has set the stage for how I observe what was, is now, and will never be again, along with the emotions that accompany this reality.

A new mindset has developed for me after you left, and this is another way I deal with my grief. Now I make a mental note with the added attention of whether this was before or after Jai died in order to locate you, my dear son, in the timeline of my life.

In spite of my ongoing grief, I will continue to culture my inner happiness in all the ways I know how, with a prayer that one day my broken heart may eventually heal.

Love,
Mom

EBB AND FLOW OF LOVE

Dear Jai,

December 25, 2020

Every moment in this timebound reality of life, there lies within, the infinite nature of timelessness, that quietly resides between the space from one point to the next.

These moments have infinity neatly packaged up, encapsulated and labeled so I can view and analyze them, but in essence I find it's just a gesture of the eternal nature of creation, going on and on and on and then pausing for a second so I can appreciate it.

In this unbounded current of creation is the ebb and flow of my love for you, for God, and everything of beauty.

Your life was, but for a brief minute, in the limitless span of eternity, but your impact has left an indelible imprint on my life.

The fullness of my love for you, my dearest son, ebbs out to the ocean of universal love and the impulse of that love flows back to me.

A graceful fluidity governs this eternal cycle of the infinite power of our love, moving from fullness to fullness as I joyfully bask in its abundance.

Love,
Mother

ANOTHER JAI SIGHTING

Dear Jai,

January 4, 2021

Kelly's childhood best friend recently contacted her about an experience she had with you the other night.

Her friend said you visited her in what she thought was a dream, but you were very much alive in spirit and present with her, and it felt like more than a dream. You had a message to give her to share with your loved ones.

She told your sister: "I had a dream last night that Jai started visiting me as his ten-year-old self. I could see him perfectly: his curly brown hair, big eyes and round face. He came to me because he wanted to go around to all the people in his life and give them messages. His energy was all love, beauty, and peace! And I always felt amazing when he was with me. On some level I thought, 'I need to remember what he is telling me so I can tell Kel when I wake up,' and of course I forgot, ...but his messages were so brilliant, profound and full of love.

I felt sad when I woke up because it felt so good to be in his presence. Not sure what it means, but he did feel like an angel. I'm going back to the image of when he was giving messages for you, Kelly, and I can hear what he said. I remember him talking about his love for you and that it's still alive. It felt enormous! Like he was showing me how big the love he had for you is. It felt warm and all-encompassing and huge."

I love you,
Mom

SONG IN MY HEART

Dear Jai,

January 7, 2021

Part of what I wish to say to you has no words, but resides in the silence of my being. I can barely express the heartfelt emotions until they begin to surface, percolating with lively excitement, and I can no longer contain myself. I am compelled to find the quintessential expressions that capture my devotion to you, dear Jai, if only in mere words.

I am the keeper of the rich legacy you left behind. A sacred duty has been bestowed on me, as your love beckons me to continue on and sing the song in my heart; the song of your beautiful life.

This is the inheritance I received from you, a worthy treasure to be honored and my way to greet each new day without you in it.

Deep sorrow and unbounded love have been woven into the tapestry of my life and the golden thread of our alliance will continue on.

Love,
Mom

YOUR MAIL

Dear Jai,

January 7, 2021

A piece of your mail arrived at our home today. When I saw the envelope, I experienced a strong sensation of loss. It came over me like a punch to my gut and in a split second I became a tidal wave of tears. In that moment the tangible presence of you was extremely strong. The person that you once were, the constant reminder of your absence from my world and the overwhelming feeling of no more Jai; it all came crashing down upon me. I haven't had an outburst of that magnitude for quite some time. I realize the sensation of your loss is now a part of me and certain incidences enliven the deep gash of pain it left behind.

Your father was also upset. He said to me that he didn't think you would want us to be sad that he died. I responded, 'How can a mother that lost her son, not respond with tears?"

Justin, I know for sure that if I had died before you did, you would be a total wreck for a long time. You were a deeply feeling man with a soft and sensitive heart. In my dying you would have lost the biggest cheerleader in your life: the person that embraced every part of who you were with no judgment. The person who carried you and pushed you out into the world.

Over the past fifteen months, several of your friends have told me you confided in them that you found it difficult to find a woman to spend your life with. You said no one measured up to your mother and sister. I was so surprised to hear this. I suppose we all have our standards of what we measure our ideals to, so I thank you for this lovely compliment.

So yes, I think if I died first, you would definitely be grieving me pretty hard, and that's okay, because it exposes the depth of our love for one another.

Love,
Mother

YOUR LINEAGE

Dear Jai,

January 15, 2021

I take great pride in being a parent and having two wonderful children: a son and a daughter. I know your Dad does as well. Even though you died, I still feel I have two children. Your death didn't erase that from me, and it never will.

Dad and I had our own individual and distinctive relationships with you. The dynamics between a mother and son differs from the father/son bond.

Growing up Italian-American, I know how important it is for a man to have a son. Male progeny comes with great certitude that the family name will be carried forward into the future generations, and the lineage will continue on. A sense of one's immortality.

Who we are today has the genetic blueprint of our ancestors. Our bloodline serves as a foundation of who and what we may become. We express the traits that were handed down to us, along with the unique signature of our individuality, shaped by behaviors and environmental input.

Physically you took after your Dad and his father in height, being over six feet tall, inheriting their long, lean physique, good balance, and athletic coordination.

You had your Dad's intellectual prowess of how to be a good businessman, and like him, you were quite successful at it. I remember the long telephone conversations you and he had when you wanted his input on a specific investment.

Both of your great grandfathers were also entrepreneurs and your maternal great grandfather did quite well for himself, owning a gas station and car repair shop. Your paternal great grandfather owned a popular barbershop and managed to take good care of his family during the Great Depression of 1929.

He took much pride in that.

Along with a good intellect, you and Dad both had clear intuition in business matters when needed. Like Dad you had a strong sense of integrity, honesty and a generous heart. Sometimes generous to a fault.

For thirty-one years your father had the good fortune in having the male extension of himself in you. Now that you have died, Dad will not witness the continuation of his son moving into the future and modeling his traits of caring for the needs of a family. He will not see his family name, the name his father passed on to him be handed down.

All of that has been cut short since you died, and the birth of a future generation of your offspring will not come to pass.

Love,
Mom

DIVINE COUNTERPART

Dear Jai,

I observe the sacredness that resides in moments that seem ordinary or uneventful. In the day-to-day routine of living, I get a glimpse of something much deeper. An understanding beyond my mind's comprehension is revealed to me.

Alongside this third dimensional world lingers something so much bigger than what meets the eye. A great, divine play acts out in the subtleties of creation. I'm thinking about you as I do my daily chores. Suddenly a celestial blue light is sparkling before me, hinting at a heavenly world that exists beyond this one.

In the stillness, I feel it.

Your death, dear Jai, has opened my awareness to the truth; every day, life walks hand in hand with its divine counterpart.

Love,
Mom

LAY CLAIM

Dear God,

                                January 17, 2021

Hi, it's me, Vicki. I wanted to remind you how hard it is for a parent to lose a child. Even on good days, the reality of this loss is hell.

I am just saying.

You came up with a brilliant plan that the human species can multiply itself through the function of procreation. You gave us the ability to produce a part of ourselves into the form of another.

You designed this miracle to take place through the biologic of a female's physiology. With the participation of the male's genetic make-up, the spark of life is ignited and this unformed being will spend the next nine months growing inside the woman's womb.

How amazing is this! Your creativity is mind boggling. It's perfection; the true meaning of a work of art.

The closeness between mother and child begins in her womb and grows stronger, deeper and richer once the human birth occurs.

When this small, vulnerable little being is ready to come out and greet the world, there's nothing more important to the child's mother, but to protect it with her life. She instinctively knows this and the father does too.

A huge part of their focus is protector of their newborn and this continues throughout life.

The family bond grows with each passing year and every milestone in their offspring's life becomes a celebratory event with an outpouring of love from family and friends and chronicled through photos, videos and cards expressing loving sentiments.

These mileposts are also a recognition that the child is still alive and thriving. They have survived illnesses, accidents and all the dangers that are lurking out there in the world.

Even though the desire for survival is strong there comes a time to surrender. In the contract of one's existence, their lease is eventually up and they must return their borrowed body and give it back to Mother Earth. This power of surrender is bigger than anything we can fathom.

Despite how much we try as a parent to thwart our child's death, we lose in the end. Hidden medical conditions, terminal diseases, accidents, and tragically suicides, come along and lay claim to our precious one.

The point of transition comes and a new reality of life without the child we protected with every ounce of our being arrives. It is time for the parent to relinquish the hold they had on their loved one, whether they like it or not.

I don't believe that a child should die before their parents, but obviously what I think has no bearing on this sad occurrence, it happens all the time.

Really God, in all your brilliance, how can you allow that to happen? In a perfect world, I am sure this wouldn't be the case.

I am just saying.

Love,
Vicki

ETERNAL FLAME

Dear Jai,

January 21, 2021

In the early morning silence, I awaken from my nighttime rest and your love comes into my heart. I lie awake in the stillness of your presence, taking you in. I ask how your time in heaven is coming along. I wonder if any new wisdom was revealed to you while I was asleep.

I keep the candles glowing for you throughout the night in my constant vigil, so you can find me in this vast creation, in the hope that the light of my love will lead the way for you back to your home, back to your family.

The glimmering light of your mother's presence and steadfast devotion is always watching out for you. It's the spark of my small earthly humanity that shines into this unbounded universe.

As you continue to journey on, may your family's love be a part of your new life, for in that spark of light is the eternal flame of our unending love for our dear Jai.

Love,
Mother

IN THE END

Dear Jai,

January 25, 2021

What is left is a memory of you: the deep love I feel, a parent's broken heart, and a mother's longing for her child. It's only natural to feel this way after such a loss.

You were a physical part of me for nine months, you can't get any closer than that to a person, and now you're gone and we can't be any further apart. These two extremes are quite excessive and I find the end of your physical reality very distracting.

When you died, I didn't set out to write a book about my grief. I wrote because I needed an outlet for my shock, to make sense of your death, and express my feelings in order to maintain some semblance of normalcy in my life, a time when nothing felt normal.

The strong desire to continue writing saved me from falling into a black hole of grief, and allowed me to face this loss and examine the life and death of my son.

I felt you cheering me on.

As the writings progressed, I wanted to continue to pay tribute to your life through the memories and insights that surfaced along the way. Your love was the impetus that moved my pen across the pages, in endless expressions of my deep sadness and unwavering devotion to you.

In the end, the golden threads of your humanity knitted together the fullness and joy that were an integral part of the fabric of your human incarnation; a fine embroidery was created. The numerous vignettes of your earthly sojourn designed the unique signature of, Justin 'Jai' Malloy, and aptly highlighted a life well lived.

Until we meet again, my dear son, remember our love for you is infinite and eternal.

Love,
Mom, Dad and Kelly

GUARDIAN OF JOY

Dear Jai,

February 1, 2021

A close friend of Kelly's and yours recently sent me a dream she had about of you. Reading this and the possibilities of what we may be doing on the other side of life broke boundaries for me. Whether this was a dream or an insight into a multidimensional reality, it had an uplifting influence; my spirits were lifted. It really fit your personality of of who you were in human form.

This is what her friend relayed to Kelly:

"Jai had visited you, Kelly, and told you many important things. Because of this, you wanted to inform everyone in your life and everyone who knew Jai, so you threw a party for your friends and family. The event took place in a big house. It reminded me of the house in Iowa you and Jai lived in with your parents. Everyone was gathered in the living room with appetizers, cookies, and beverages. It was a huge celebration. You stood at the front of the room to tell us everything.

Kel, you told us that when he visited you, he told you that he had a new name. The name was inherently so full of joy and humor that when you told everyone his new name you started laughing so hard with pure joy and so did everyone in the crowd. He said that he was working with a new kind of life form in a different solar system. He would arrive with a group of dimensional beings and his job was to oversee, assist, assess and report on how much joy they were experiencing. He was a guardian angel for this other solar system. When you told us the stories he shared with you (that now I can't remember) they were full of joy and humor. You and all of us in the crowd just couldn't stop giggling and smiling. He infused you with the joy he was now in charge of in his solar system. You were so excited to share all of this information. You had a very, very long visit and he told you many stories. You told us that he looked the same in a lot of ways: his brown wavy hair, huge smile, and bright eyes; this made your heart happy. He had a prestigious role in his solar system. It was a very important job and high up in his system's organizational structure. What a huge responsibility to oversee the joy in all the lives! His responsibilities were also to intervene, when necessary, in their lives to make sure they were experiencing enough joy. And he was loving it. His job was ONLY to make sure their lives were full of joy. That was all he wanted. He wanted laughter, dancing and fun. He made sure playfulness was taking place in his solar system. By contacting you, he infused you with that same feeling. And then by you sharing all the information with everyone in the crowd, you infused us with the same playfulness! The group of people you were talking to (myself included) was howling with laughter and so jolly. I remember not being able to stop laughing. Bubbling bliss. He infused you with bubbling bliss, and then you infused us with bubbling bliss."

Gosh Jai, what a fun filled, incredible dream!

Love,
Mom

TRANSCENDENTAL LOVE

Dear Jai,

As I revel in the boundless pleasure of transcendental love, my arms are open wide.

I discover the beauty in letting go, as I continue to write your ending, a composition of my sorrow that leads me to your joy.

Our story is steeped in love. Its profundity is beyond what my limited mind can fathom, but the subtle sense of your immortality lives on in me. You breathe life into me. I draw strength from you.

I ask God to please hold my hand as I journey on, so there are no missteps, no blunders along the way. And when I come back home to you, there will be no regrets, just transcendental love.

Love,
Mom

YEAR TWO—THE PRESENCE
OF YOUR ABSENCE

Dear Jai,

August 5, 2021

It has been two years since you passed away and left for heaven. The tragic occurrence of your death continues to sit with me. The deep longing and constant ache of missing you, my dear son, is still quite strong.

Your Grandmother Malloy recently passed away. Have you run across her somewhere in the heavens? We went back East for her funeral services. It was a full and rich experience to honor her life and many accomplishments, especially in the raising of her eight amazing children.

To grieve my mother-in-law, who was elderly and in a state of decline for several years, was very different from the grief of losing you. You were in the prime of your life and full of so much energy and passion to continue living. It would have appeared to many of us that you didn't have the time to die. You had a lot more of life to live, but obviously God had other plans for you.

Going to your Grandmother's funeral triggered the memory of your services, and the sting of your death was provoked once again. Your sister and I sobbed the whole time.

In my mind's eye I could see you standing next to me in the Church where Grandma's mass was being performed. You would have come to pay your respects to her, and afterwards spent time with your cousins and shared with them what you have been up to these past couple of years.

You would have been in the warmth and comfort of your family, but instead the presence of your absence was profoundly felt.

Love always,
Mother

TODAY IS YOUR BIRTHDAY

Dear Jai,

August 11, 2021

We shared an unconditional love with one another. I felt an acceptance and deep respect from you since the time you were my little boy. From your innocent childlike hugs and kisses to your adult embraces, a bond that was unbreakable and a love that was invincible was always present. That feeling still remains even though you now live in the afterlife.

Today marks the auspicious day of what would have been your thirty-fourth birthday.

I am going over to your memorial site in the sunshine of a new morning. Butterflies are flying along the path I'm walking on. The wild grasses planted around your space are majestically standing at attention and gently swaying in the warm summer breeze. I place red roses on the large boulder that has a plaque attached to it, etched with heartfelt words of adoration to you. I sit on the dragonfly-designed benches taking in the moment with the sun warming my skin.

On this day, you my friend have come home to me, if only for a short visit. I sit with you in the beauty of nature to honor a time that once was, and ponder where I find myself now as you reside in the heavens.

Happy Birthday, my dear love.

Love,
Mother

I LOVE YOU

Dear Jai,

I haven't been doing much writing to you lately. I feel so much of what I needed to express to you in the first year and a half of your passing has been said.

Perhaps there is more to say...

Maybe it doesn't always have to be profound insights, sweet stories, or clever rhymes, but maybe just saying, "I love you," is plenty.

I love you.

Love,
Mom

NOT AVAILABLE

Dear Jai,

September 16, 2021

I called your cell phone today. The recording said, "The wireless customer you are calling is not available. Please try again later." Then I called again and it said, "The number you are calling is not a working number." I played it over several times. I realize to have a message regarding the status of your availability, or lack thereof, from your former cell phone, is a faint part of you. Some remnants of your time as a human being are lingering, and I like that. It made me feel good, as though you were still alive. I sit and bask in the warm feeling of you, dear Justin.

I guess I'm not surprised that your number hasn't been given to someone else.

No one can ever take your place.

Love,
Mom

THE WEIGHT

Dear Jai,

September 17, 2021

Gosh, grief is heavy. It weighs on me. I have changed. A part of myself is gone: a void that needs filling, an endless yearning for your life to be returned to you as my son, Justin. Life would be so much fuller if you were alive!

I'm still not ready to attend celebratory events. I would feel like a hypocrite trying to be all festive and merry, while I am in a state of deep mourning. I hope that one day I can shed the weight of grief and get back to a permanent place of true happiness.

I realize your death is now part of my history. Losing you is an integral part of the life I am living in this century. As imperfect as my life seems, now that you've died, I must assume that this is beneficial to my story: the journey of me.

I hope to do a better job of embracing life with all of its imperfections and that one day I can say, "It was all perfect."

I still need your guidance.

Love,
Mom

WHO WOULD HAVE THOUGHT...?

Dear Justin,

September 21, 2021

Who would have thought that one day Dad would take ownership of your much-loved Tundra truck? He would have sold his Jeep to take on the care and maintenance of one of your earthly possessions left behind, and every time we would drive in your truck, we feel the spirit of Justin is with us.

Who would have thought that the pen and ink dragonfly drawing you drew at fourteen years old, and I had framed and sent to you, would one day be mine, hanging on my bedroom wall?

Who would have thought the blue sapphire ring you never took off your finger would be handed to me in a plastic bag as part of your remains from the E.R. doctor? Your abandoned ring would find a new home sitting on my gold-plated platter with other mementos symbolizing my love for you.

Who would have thought that a dear friend would take your precious Rudraksha beads on a spiritual pilgrimage to various holy and sacred spots in India? Blessings would accumulate in your name, for your family as well, and I would have the framed photos of their journey hanging in my meditation room.

Who would have thought that you would suddenly die at thirty-one years of age? That your ashes would be scattered in special places you grew up in, and the bulk of your remains distributed into the holy Ganges River. Dad's friend, along with a Hindu priest, would be present to perform sacred rituals and chant special prayers for your soul's journey.

Who would have thought that before Dad and I would die, you

would breathe your last breath? A lovely memorial site would be erected near the home of your youth and a second one at the local animal shelter. Places of honor would be designed especially for you as a tribute to show how much you were loved and respected.

Who would have thought...?

Love always,
Mother

I HAD A DREAM

Dear Jai,

October 9, 2021

I had a dream about you last night. You, Dad, Kelly and myself were all together at a wedding. I noticed that no one was speaking to you, nor were you interacting with anyone. It suddenly dawned on me it was because you had died and only your family was able to see you. You were quietly by our side during the event. You felt so real and it was absolutely fantastic to be with you in spirit, which looked human to us.

The dream was a gift from you and I am grateful for that moment of seeing and feeling you.

I love you so very much,
Mom

SCROLLING THROUGH THE YEARS

Dear Jai,

October 9, 2021

I was scrolling through my cell phone calendar for something unrelated to your death. I was going back in years when I started to get a slight twinge in my body that began to pulsate. Each year I was moving past became a trigger to the amount of time you had left to live. I had to stop when I reached 2015. At that point it hit me quite hard that you would only be alive for four more years. I scrolled forward toward your death day of 2019, well by then I was a bucket of tears.

It's Saturday morning and I'm lying in bed reading our conversations from old texts we sent to one another. I'm watching some of the videos you sent of your travels to places you visited in Northern California, a tour of your new home in Sacramento, and a walk through of an RV you were considering purchasing.

As I read our silent conversations, I hear your voice in the words you are sending me and feel the emotions they generate. There is much love in our dialogue.

In one of the texts I told you I had organized a Vedic ceremony performed by Eastern Indian priests to petition the gods to give you, Kel, Dad and me long lives: assurance of our longevity. These petitions are something like doing the Rosary in Catholicism, in the sense they ask God for special protection and graces for ourselves and loved ones. You died two months later. Obviously some things are destined to be and nothing can intervene.

Three months before you died, you took a trip with some friends to Spain. You sent me videos and photos of this country.

Upon arriving in Spain, you walked around the city of Barcelona taking in the sites.

You said, "It's the most beautiful city I've ever been to. The churches are like nothing I've seen. The ornate architecture and stained-glass windows are gorgeous. The streets are lined with palm trees and very clean. We went to a two-hundred-year-old bar that was a favorite hangout of the famous painter, Pablo Picasso. Here is a photo of dust encrusted bottles of alcohol sitting on a shelf from that period of time. This country is warm and welcoming; it feels magical. I'm so inspired and amazed by the culture. I hope our family can go on some special adventures together some day. Love you mamma."

None of these hopes and dreams will ever come true.

Scrolling through the memories of our loving conversations brought you back home to me. Even though I'm feeling like a limp rag from sobbing my eyes out, I love to feel your human side. I miss the personality of Justin, and if I can experience a part of that for a few minutes, then good!

I'm grateful I have access to your humanity and can still scroll through memory lane with you my dear son.

I love you,
Mother

I AM JUST REFLECTING

Dear Jai,

I smile when I think that you were once here as a human being, as I am. We had a human connection. Even though you no longer have a physical body, your humanity lives on within me. Your cells are a part of me along with your feelings, impressions and awareness; they are still lively in my consciousness. We are related to one another and nothing, not even death, can alter that.

When you were an Earthling, a personality we called Jai, you were filled with so much love, playfulness and lots of energy. I am sure you continue to embody those qualities, just in a different form.

After your death I was angry at the world. I now realize that knowing you were here, for however brief your time was, the world can't be all wrong because in this world was you.

You now reside in the space of timelessness, while I reside in the place of time. Is it possible to elevate me so our contrasting realities and my deep sadness can be washed away by the flow of eternity?

I am reflecting back to when you were a child. You had golden highlights in your hair and they would glisten in the sunlight. Since you have been gone, I am wondering if golden glitters of heavenly light are playing off your celestial hair?

Jai, are you floating in sparkles of light as you are immersed in the radiance of God's love?

I am just reflecting.

I love you,
Mom

REMINDERS

Dear Jai,

October 18, 2021

I took down your photos. Everything is still up in your bedroom, but the photos I have of you on the entryway table and my nightstand have been put away. They were constantly in my range of vision and I couldn't look at them without feeling a huge pinch. The incessant reminder of your death became too much. I need a break from crying.

I'm sorry.

I have several vases of flowers in place of your photos and battery-operated candles are continuously glowing representing my endless love for you.

Now you are being honored in a subtle form without your human appearance being on display. Actually, it seems more appropriate since you are no longer bound by your physical appearance. An array of colorful flowers representing nature and the essence of light, which we are made of, are paying tribute to our dear, Jai.

I love you,
Mom

MORE GROUNDED

Dear Jai,

October 25, 2021

These days I'm starting to feel grounded and overall stronger. It doesn't mean I have stopped grieving, but it's less than where I was in the early days of your passing. Perhaps I'll have a big melt down eventually, but for today the tears are light trickles running down my face.

I realize that after two years of your death, when I do heavily grieve you, it allows me to feel more connected to you. The grief gets me in touch with the person, Justin, that I am remembering and missing. When I'm not grieving, you feel far away: a faint thought, a distant memory. I don't like you feeling like a faint or distant memory. I need to feel you close by.

It's still hard at times to believe that you died and that your human form has been reduced to ashes that have been dispersed in lakes, rivers, oceans, and planted in the ground. It may take a lifetime to adjust to this reality.

Your sister is home for the week. I am grateful that the trauma of your death has not impacted our relationship with her. I've heard how some families are so broken by the passing of a child that the severity of the loss alters the relationship of the family dynamic permanently.

We are still a close and loving family and that is my joy.

I love you,
Mom

OLD AGE

My dear Jai,

As I'm growing older, I feel my body is shifting and aging and the flexibility I once had is waning. I still have pretty good energy and I can move quickly, but I see the changes that are taking place as part of the natural progression of this phase of life for someone that is pushing seventy years of age. I continue to go on walks and stretch every day to help slow down this process.

Inside I feel like a sixteen-year-old girl excited for a hug and kiss from your father, having fun designing labels for my hand sanitizers, (something that developed out of the pandemic), and going on outings with my girlfriends for a day of beauty treatments. Engaging in activities that stir my inner youthfulness is a good way to stay young in spirit.

I recently came across a video of you, Nana and myself. You were home visiting me for Mother's Day, and we just came back from brunch. The video shows you and I each holding onto to Nana's hands as we are lending our support to her as she struggles to walk. She was close to ninety-three years of age. It's a sweet moment captured in time. Six weeks later she passed away.

Watching this video I realized that when I get really old, I won't have your hand to hold to help me walk. I won't have your arm to rest against as my strength starts to weaken. I won't have you nearby cheering me on if the going gets tough. You won't be here with me in my old age. That makes me very sad. The burden will be on your sister. I sure hope I don't become a burden on anyone, but it would have been nice to have you here for so many reasons.

I love you so much,
Mother

STUMBLING THROUGH

Dear Jai,

October 29, 2021

Tonight my mind was full of remembering you and your childhood friends. You always seemed to have many good buddies at every stage of your development. One of those friends bought a facility in town and turned it into a dance club. Your sister is home for a visit and will be going out tomorrow evening to the club. I know for sure if you were home, you would be joining in the festivities. You would connect with an old friend and enjoy seeing one another as grown adults. I can see it all so clearly, and I hear your voice as well. You would be here with us continuing your life.

I'm brought back to who you were and what might have been if you didn't die. Such an emotional dilemma I find myself in. I cried and cried with these thoughts and feelings weighing heavy on my heart, stimulating my tears to fall.

I found myself stumbling through a passage of time.

I love you,
Mom

RARE AND PRECIOUS

Dear Jai,

October 31, 2021

It is hard to live without you. The most cherished part of myself has been stripped away from me when you died.

We all loved everything about you and that is why your death is so very difficult to accept. It truly is a huge loss that all your loved ones have suffered.

Your sister's visit home was incredibly nourishing for your family. The love and closeness we share is still strong and stable.

The last day she was home she decided to go into your room to see and feel the brother she once had. Your room is a quiet sanctuary dedicated to your life and all the memorabilia you left behind. Your drawings and photos on display play a significant role for us in preserving your memory and enliven your personality. She became quite emotional and exited the room sobbing. You were her dearest friend and brother and it hurts this sensitive woman so deeply not to have you around anymore.

She, like myself, will probably never ever get over this loss and the relationships we each had with you. The depth of our love for you is transcendent and to lose something so rare and precious took a big piece out of our lives.

This has made life more challenging. Our happiness waxes and wanes, especially when the traumatic memory of your death is enlivened.

Love,
Mom

MOURNING SEASON

Dear Jai,

November 6, 2021

Life continues on. Each passing day comes and goes. Some days are easier than others. There is no rhyme or reason to my grief; it is what it is. Happy and sad, up and down. A big jumble of emotions and feelings running through me. Writing helps, so does going out of town for the day and getting absorbed in a good movie.

We will feel your absence this holiday year, especially during Christmastime. Getting through the pain of your absence with a smile on my face and putting one foot in front of the other so I can continue moving forward, is how life seems to go along. We move through the turn of the seasons as we push the clocks back tomorrow for daylight savings time.

I'm still in the mourning season of my life.

Love,
Mom

SOFT CUSHION

Dear Jai,

November 8, 2021

I didn't realize when you were alive how much your life, love and presence filled me. Probably because it was always there. It was a natural part of me, like my eyes, arms, heart and so on. From giving birth to you, you automatically became a part of my physical make-up and essential to my motherhood. The love we have for our children fills us like nothing else ever can.

Since you died, it's as though the stuffing has been knocked out of me. The soft cushion of being your mother and the unconditional love that we shared is gone. No more padding to shield me from life's traumas. Without this buffer I feel more of everything. My skin is thinner and I feel every prick and poke of life's pains.

Your death has also given me a depth of love, compassion, and empathy that is so much richer in the fabric of my life. The comfortable nesting cocoon of your presence, my dear son, is gone, but my love for you has transcended beyond anything my heart has ever known.

I love you,
Mom

MEMORY TRAILS

Dear Jai,

The recent murder of our high school Spanish teacher coupled with the death by Russian roulette of a young man in our community has deeply disturbed me. I immediately had a strong impulse to call and talk to you about the insanity that is taking place in my town. We would talk when I was upset about something and the impulse to speak with you was a natural reaction.

I need your input, some consolation and words of wisdom, but you aren't here to communicate with me in this way. I want your perspective, which was always so expanded and wise.

The depth of this connection with you and what we once shared is still quite strong. It has left an impression on me. A lasting imprint on my life. These memory trails lead me home to you, my son. There are many of these trails that bring me back to you. Fine threads of our connectivity, weaving us together like an embroidered cloth on the backdrop of my life.

I really miss you.

Love,
Mom

STEADFAST DEVOTION

Dear Jai,

November 26, 2021

Seated on the summit of creation I gain a panoramic view of where I have been residing since you died. I find myself at the threshold of here to there. The unseen, invisible world is felt within my grasp. I live on the edge as my life continues on in a state of silent reflection.

Shaken out of my small existence, I am facing the reality of the inevitable; so close is my home. A universe where you, my dear son, and my loved ones that left before you have passed through time into the arms of the timeless. You have broken free of the confines of the world I am presently in and have entered into the beyond.

There is nothing left for me to do but be in the grace of continual prayer: the prayer of my unending love riding on the wings of my steadfast devotion to you.

I love you,
Mom

FEELING HUMAN

Dear Justin,

December 1, 2021

Your death was an abrupt wake-up call of how intense the human experience can become. All of the emotions and feelings that I've always had, have significantly intensified. Feelings of love, loss, grief, sadness, shock, gratitude, empathy and compassion have gained a depth of experience that has grown out of mourning your death. Love and grief are horsemen riding alongside of one another and grow deeper with each and every tear that I shed, not only for you, but for all of humanity.

These intensified emotions have spilled over into my life and I feel these daily occurrences profoundly. There is no more hiding. I am a fully exposed human being, naked and unabashed, responding to what the world presents. Everyday living is perceived as a much bigger event now that you are gone.

My heart is tender and I have become extremely sensitized to these currents running through me.

This is where I find myself two-and-a-half years after your life on Earth has ended.

I love you,
Mom

YOU FREED ME

Dear Jai,

December 27, 2021

You broke my heart wide open, and all I can feel is my love, all I can feel is your love, but I can't deny that I know it is really...one love.

I will continue on, and carry the flaming torch of our love forward and into the future. This is the endowment you bequeathed to me as our love grows stronger and richer with each passing day.

In some crazy way, the pain of your death has liberated my heart and has allowed it to open even wider than I thought possible. You have given me the permission to let go. Although you are gone from my life, your presence remains and is felt more than ever.

What are these shenanigans the universe is presenting me with? What is this game of life and death that I am completely captivated by?

With open arms I am holding on to you, for in my surrendered heart is where I find my dear child, Jai.

You have freed me.

Love always,
Mom

I LOVE FLOWERS

Dear Justin,

January 2, 2022

You knew how much I loved flowers and always gave me the biggest and most magnificent floral arrangements for special occasions.

Flowers are graceful creatures, elevating everything around them with their vibrant presence. They adorn the space wherever they are placed with selfless beauty. My dear flowers where would the Earth be without you? You reflect a heavenly place. I gaze upon you and see the promise of a kinder, gentler world.

I breathe in your fragrance and my senses are elevated. I am captivated by your ethereal qualities. You're too delicate for this harsh world, and yet you keep on growing and blossoming into thousands of different varieties in a rainbow of colors: pink roses, burgundy orchids, orange lilies, and yellow sunflowers. I'm dazzled by your infinite range of shades and shapes.

You are the epitome of fullness, of reaching your highest potential with the aid of sunshine and water. You have made the journey from seed to blossom. Once you reach your peak, you go back to rest in your dormant state until a seed grows you once more, and you come back to greet a brand-new day.

I love you, my dear flowers.

Love,
Mom

PERPETUAL LOVE

Dear Jai,

Pardon me, but I've been busy writing my tragedy. What does this mean for me? How does this change the way I see and what is to be?

In letting go, I discover boundless delight in surrendering my pain and the most profound hurt this mother could possibly feel: the loss of you, my beloved child, and yet I find your beauty in my sorrow.

I'm still dreaming of our past, but you didn't last and you had no time for the future.

Jumping into my pool of tears I uncover a love so deep that I can never emerge from it, nor do I wish to.

Loving you in the depths of my sorrow, I rise up floating in the ocean of perpetual love.

I love you,
Mom

RELEASE AND SURRENDER

Dear Jai,

January 12, 2022

I continue with my daily exercises of stretching, pulling and pushing my joints and muscles. I notice that my grief is sitting quietly, stored away in the nooks and crannies of my body. It begins to reveal itself as my tear drops start to fall from these repetitive motions. The tension in my body is loosening up as I proceed to push and squeeze it to keep myself limber. As this activity continues, I see how much my mind and body are intimately connected. The impact of your death left its emotional imprint not only in my heart, but the emotions have lodged themselves in my joints, muscles, tendons, organs, cells, and every part of me.

Your death is a tsunami washing through every fiber of my being.

Today my sorrow is moving out through my shoulder exercises. The burden of grief that I carry around finds some relief. I feel like a lump of dough being kneaded, formed and made pliable in order to create more flow and circulation. I find that the movements and grief are working in unison, kneading my physical mass. Sometimes it's gently caressing, and other times deeply pinching and stretching every nerve. I liberate the residual trauma of your passing as I continue to press upon my physical form, and my body relinquishes more grief.

Grieving moves at its own pace. It's a steady, lively process of release, gently happening in its own time as I continue to surrender my tears and pay tribute to your life.

I love you,
Mom

LEGACY OF LOVE

Dear Jai,

January 26, 2022

We are moving into the third year of your transition and it is clear to me that I am going to deeply miss you for the rest of my life. Your transition is also my transition as I navigate my way through my senior years without you, my dear son.

In my memory resides the persistent imprint that your death has left behind. It is my constant companion. Sometimes this memory sits quietly in my awareness and the understanding that this is the way it was meant to be brings a sense of peace. There are other times I feel flat and void of any emotion of your loss, and there are moments when I am incredibly sad and the loss of your life is a bitter potion to swallow. In that state of emotion, it doesn't matter what I believe in because my heart is broken and I need to have a good cry.

Since you died, I have a strong need to keep this ongoing dialogue alive so I can stay connected to you in the way that I know how. Perhaps this is your way of holding your mother's hand as I walk along the path of life without you. I'm sure you know that expressing my love to you is a natural part of my motherhood, and writing has been a great outlet for me to clarify my feelings from the trauma in the aftermath of your death.

My unending supplications and heartfelt petitions have been birthed into a book of our love. From years of writing to you, a memoir of our life was born and the interweaving of the passages of our time together formed a lovely narrative. The interconnectedness of who we are and the depth of our love became apparent to me, and has inspired me to keep writing.

As words continue to find their way onto this page, I am reminded how brief our sojourn on this planet is; you proved that. Time here is a minute long in comparison to the eternal nature of infinity. This is my stopping off point before my next adventure, one that you have embarked on before me. I truly believe we will be reunited once again, and the legacy of our love will carry on.

I love you,
Mom

THE GOLDEN CORD

Dear Jai,

January 27, 2022

As my mind is constantly probing into the wonders of life, I'm remembering when I was pregnant with you. No matter how much time has passed since your birth to your eventual death, the umbilical cord of our connectivity continues to linger. Even though early on the navel string is cut, the imprint of that connection is the conduit which attaches us in the most profound way. I feel this powerful bond that forms between a mother and her child is part of the uniqueness of the mother/child relationship: the golden thread that binds us. This supportive and nurturing link is integral to the unending love we have for each other. Is this cord the creator's metaphor to demonstrate how united we are, and this cosmic thread is what links us together on earth and continues into the heavens?

Since you died, I find myself waking up to the absolute genius of the creator's mind and the sheer perfection of how It orchestrates every infinite facet of creation. I am humbled with profound gratitude and admiration as I gain a panoramic view of Its brilliance.

In the end the finest feeling of our love for one another, the invisible golden cord of our alliance as mother and son is what keeps our souls connected and hearts flowing.

I'll continue to ride the wave of our love and surrender to wherever it takes me.

Love,
Mom

I LOVE YOU INTO INFINITY

Dear Jai,

I loved you on Earth,
I love you in heaven,
I will love you into infinity.
My love is with you wherever you are.
My love for you is always growing;
it cannot be contained, bound or stifled.
The essence of my love is love and it comes
in different forms:
love for God, husband, children, parents,
family, friends, siblings, animals, nature,
ad infinitum
If I had the choice, I would never let you go.
You were my baby boy, my one and only son;
you were a happy child.
Now that I have lost you, I will
wait for us to experience heaven
together.
Until then I will sing my adorations
to you, to God, and to the universe.

My song of love is my song for you.

I love you,
Mom

BEDTIME STORIES

Dear Jai,

I'm lying awake in bed. My mind is restless. Many thoughts, feelings and images of you are moving through my awareness. Beginning in infancy to adulthood, the movie reel of your life plays on. I'm holding you as my newborn baby, then our final hug six weeks before your passing. We are following the script that was written and playing our roles perfectly.

Today would have been your 35th birthday.

I get up to find my manuscript of letters I have been journaling to you these past three years. I begin reading them and my mind starts to settle down. Soft, loving expressions that I continuously write to you, soothe me. I enjoy reading the journey of your life from birth to death to afterlife. It's quite a ride navigating the depths of my despair to the culmination of our transcendental love. I continue to experience the extensive range of human emotions. A fullness in my heart is forming. It encompasses a grander scale of life, as this profound love for you keeps growing and developing me as a person.

I feel you are here, alongside me, reading my bedtime stories of our time as mother and son.

I'm starting to feel sleepy. I turn the lamp off and my heart is nourished as I gently fall into a deep slumber.

Good-night my son.

I love you,
Mom

ESSENTIAL REMEMBRANCES OF UNIVERSAL GRIEF, LOVE AND CELEBRATION

"When you were my child, I held you in
my arms, now that you are gone, I hold
you in my heart."

"No matter what form you are, in or out of
the human body, one thing that remains
the same—our love for one another, it is
infinite and eternal."

"Memories of our life together are passing
through my awareness in snippets of time
as they melt away into the great continuum
of infinity."

"Every moment of each day is moment
of loving you."

"A parents' grief comes from the most profound
part of what their humanity can feel. We
are united in our grief, and the
unending love we have for our departed
children."

"Everything beautiful in this world is a reminder
of your beauty."

"On the highway of life, as the winds of change
shift directions over and over again, I know that
our love is the one constant."

"Your essence, divinity, and soul lives on."

"Your love resides in the sacred space of my heart."

"The design of my life and our love is constantly fixed in my memory."

"My song of love is my song for you."

"Life has given me the breath to breathe your essence into my heart and that sustains me."

"The lovely fragrance from the blossoming rose is the sweet perfume of a mother's love for her child."

"The most beautiful ensemble I wear is this chain of love, it is the infinite thread that links our souls for all eternity."

"I honor your unique life that once was."

"Grieving you is loving you."

"Our children's memories are our sacred treasures that we keep close to us—like priceless, precious gems that we are proud to possess."

"Your life was like a beautiful tapestry of threads woven together, creating a magnificent embroidery."

"This heart of mine will never stop loving you. It will never stop beating for you; this heart of mine is always breathing you."

"I carry on wearing the finery of your love with
great pride and dignity."

"We are timeless and unbounded souls housed
in the architecture of a human body."

"From infinity to the point of our created
incarnation, our souls aligned. The powerful
force of love brought us into each other's
world and will again, someday, someway."

"Love is the nectar pouring from my heart,
my libation to the creator to give us a brand
new start."

"In this unbounded current of life is the ebb
and flow of our love."

"The fullness of my love for you flows out to the
ocean of universal love, and the impulse of that
love flows back to me."

"The spark of the divine is what animates all
humans and allows us to feel love, sadness,
joy, and everything that is part of our humanity.
It is a beautiful gift, which can deeply hurt as well."

"Part of what I wish to say has no words, but
resides in the silence of my being."

"There is a graceful fluidity in the eternal cycle
of the infinite power of our love moving from
heart to heart as I joyfully bask in its abundance."

"You are a worthy treasure to be honored and
my way to greet each new day."

"As I revel in the boundless pleasure of transcendental love, my arms are open wide."

"Loving you in the depths of my sorrow, I rise up floating in the ocean of perpetual love."

"Please hold my hand to help me walk along the path of life without you."

"With open arms I am holding onto you, for in my surrendered heart is where I find my dear child."

"The legacy of our love will continue on."

"I am here to represent you and give voice to your memory."

"Your transition is also my transition, as I learn to navigate my life without you."

"The umbilical cord of our connectivity is the golden thread that binds us on Earth and into the heavens."

"Beginnings and endings are really an illusion, for we are the ones that mark the boundaries from start to finish in order to create an orderly sequence in the events of life, and through it all the infinite stream of our love moves forward transcending this illusion we call time."

"Love is the silent voice that unifies our hearts. Love is the eternal thread that links our souls. Love is the sacred space where we hold our dear children."

SPECIAL THANKS

To all my wonderful friends and family that have given their heart and soul to my family and me during this very difficult time. Your love was the cushion to help soften the heavy blow of losing our dear son, Jai. There are no words to express my deep appreciation for all you have done for us.

To 1st World Publishing, Rodney Charles. Thank-you for believing in this book. You have no idea what this means to me.

Thanks to Jason Schneider for your encouragement to have my tribute book to Jai published. You made my heart sing!

Thank-you Nancy Gibson. You were an absolute joy to work with in the editing of this book.

My dear buddy Kay Geier. What a great friend you are. Thank-you for your patience in reading and rereading over and over with me the passages in the book and being my sounding board. You're the best!

To my dear Ed, my husband of the past thirty-nine years. We have been through many challenging situations together, and through it all our love has endured.

My beautiful daughter, Kelly. I am so sorry for your broken heart. May the healing salve of God's love mend it and make it whole once more.

To my dear son, Justin, Jai. What a journey we are on. I look forward to reuniting with you once again and until then please keep in touch. And remember our love is infinite and eternal.

Love,
Mom

ABOUT THE AUTHOR

Vicki Reccasina-Malloy lives in a small town in Iowa with her husband, Ed and cat Sunny. She has been practicing Transcendental Meditation for the past forty-six years. She loves to draw, paint, cook, be out in nature, read, spend time with friends and family especially her daughter, Kelly and pup India.

She was involved in the healing arts for ten years until life shifted her focus and direction.

She tries to be aware of the bigger picture that life is presenting and to know that in the end, everything is the way it is meant to be.

With a full heart of unending gratitude to Divine Mother and Her continued guidance.

READER APPRECIATION FOR
HEARTS OF LIGHT

"Reading this beautiful tribute to Justin, I experienced joy, sadness and healing of my own loss..."

"This book is a journal of love letters. It's a chronicle of a grieving mother's way to help cope with the death of her son, Jai, who died very suddenly and much too young. Reading the book, I felt like the chair was pulled out from under me at times, because of the depth of vulnerability, love and raw beauty that was being shared. It was like a sacred glimpse of something so personal and private that was born out of grief and then blossomed and channeled through a love that has transcended beyond what was present when Jai was alive. I think the author has a perspective and depth of wisdom that many of us who walk this life, ever get to experience. This book for me was not what you would call a page turner. It's something I could only read in small doses because it stirred up so many layers and levels of emotions. It was a humbling experience for me to have the opportunity to share in a mother's adoring love for a son that has passed on and who was also my precious, nephew."

"I imagine a dear friend handing me a shoe box from her attic, full of letters that she had written to her son after he died. Time had passed, but each letter took me to a moment, a memory that felt completely present. Delving into such an intimate treasure needs time to be savored. The letters are full of love of family that connect me with the memories of my own. Our stories convey our feelings at that time, then feelings evolve as we move through the layers of healing. I remember pulling up to a traffic light by the post office in our town. I looked in my rear-view mirror and saw my friend Vicki in the car behind me with a handsome young man at her side: her beautiful, beloved son, Jai."

"Vicki's testimonial of love to her son, Jai, is an inspiration for us all. It's not the words that I was left with, but the stitching together of a mother's and son's heart that spans beyond time and space. Every nugget she writes is sublime and melted my heart. Each vignette has its own color and flavor and transitions to the next and held my attention. I just wanted to read on as my heart expanded with unfathomable love for my godson, Jai."

CPSIA information can be obtained
at www.ICGtesting.com
Printed in the USA
BVHW070954080223
658056BV00001B/60